WE WERE RICH
AND WE DIDN'T
KNOW IT

WE WERE RICH AND WE DIDN'T KNOW IT

A Memoir of My Irish Boyhood

Tom Phelan

GALLERY BOOKS

New York London Toronto Sydney New Delhi

G

Gallery Books
An Imprint of Simon & Schuster, Inc.
1230 Avenue of the Americas
New York, NY 10020

First Gallery Books hardcover edition March 2019

GALLERY BOOKS and colophon are registered trademarks of Simon & Schuster, Inc.

For information about special discounts for bulk purchases, please contact Simon & Schuster Special Sales at 1-866-506-1949 or business@simonandschuster.com.

The Simon & Schuster Speakers Bureau can bring authors to your live event. For more information or to book an event, contact the Simon & Schuster Speakers Bureau at 1-866-248-3049 or visit our website at simonspeakers.com.

Interior design by Jaime Putorti

Manufactured in the United States of America

10 9 8 7 6 5 4 3 2 1

Library of Congress Cataloging-in-Publication Data is available.

ISBN 978-1-5011-9709-3
ISBN 978-1-5011-9711-6 (ebook)

To my sisters

In loving memory of
Annie, JohnJoe, and my brothers

CONTENTS

WE WERE RICH
AND WE DIDN'T
KNOW IT

AUTHOR'S NOTE

We Were Rich and We Didn't Know It presents my own recollections. I understand that others may have memories of the events described here that are different from my own. Some names and characteristics have been changed, and some of the dialogue has been re-created.

For readers unfamiliar with the Irish vernacular or farming terms, a glossary is provided on page 201.

JOHNJOE'S CLEVER PLAN

In the early 1930s, my father, JohnJoe Phelan, having borne the dictatorship of his father until the old man died and having buried his aged mother in the local cemetery two years later, became the master of his own destiny and the owner of a farm in Laragh, one-half mile from the town of Mountmellick in County Laois.

Mointeach Milic, which the British corrupted to Mountmellick, means the "marshy land beside the bog." JohnJoe's farm was fifty-two boggy acres that, as he himself said, were so soft they could be tilled with the belt of a blackthorn bush.

A few years before his parents died, JohnJoe began planning for his future. He knew that upon their deaths, he would have to get his sister, Molly, out of the house so he could bring in a new mistress—a wife. He already had his eye on Annie Hayes, a young woman who lived on the far end of the town in a cottage on the edge of the marsh but still in the bog.

JohnJoe was a good planner; he had a plan.

His distant cousin Kate Larkin, an aged spinster living in the townland of Aganloo, was the sole survivor of a farm-owning family.

Kate was also related to JohnJoe's uncle Pake Nugent, whom JohnJoe disliked immensely. "Pake's nothing but a land grabber!" he would snipe.

With the future relocation of Molly on his mind and Kate Larkin within a death rattle of the grave, JohnJoe bought a strawberry-jam Swiss roll and set off one Sunday morning in his pony-and-trap to travel the eight miles to Aganloo. Upon arrival, he made tea for Kate and himself, then sweetened his cousin's toothless mouth with the Swiss roll. "Ah, JohnJoe," she said, "this cake is nice and aisy on me oul gums."

JohnJoe went down on one knee before the ailing woman. "Sure, Kate, I have a favor to ask of ye. I'll have a hard time getting a wife as long as Molly is living at home with me. Would ye ever think of leaving yer house and farm to her?"

Kate generously told him to arise. "JohnJoe, I'll be changing me will tomorrow, and when I'm wearing me shroud, this place will be Molly's. I'm just sorry I'll miss yer weddin."

JohnJoe sliced the rest of the Swiss roll and placed it on a chair convenient to his benefactress. Then he set out for home, his success bearing him up. But as his pony trotted down Kate Larkin's avenue, he met Pake Nugent coming up the road on his rattling bike. John-Joe assumed that Pake, with five sons and four daughters, was about to ask Kate for her farm.

"Did you bring her anything, Pake?" JohnJoe called. "I brought her a Swiss roll."

"Maybe she'll give me a bit," Pake shouted back.

"It'll be the only thing she can give you!"

JohnJoe could not contain himself, and he roared out laughter as loud as the bawl of a mare ass.

Not long after JohnJoe's visit to Aganloo, old Kate breathed her last, and soon Molly immigrated to the Larkin farm, JohnJoe driving his horse-and-cart with beds, mattresses, and a few other sticks. His sister drove on ahead in the pony-and-trap; Molly would not be seen in a horse's cart in close proximity to an equine arse. After all, she was now a landowner.

Free of his sister, JohnJoe wiped the muck and the cow dung off his wellingtons and set about entrapping Annie Hayes in his amorous plans.

JOHNJOE GETS A WIFE

On the day JohnJoe Phelan and Annie Hayes met at a camogie game, they were not total strangers. Both belonged to the Gaelic League, and at a language class in the Mountmellick Boys School one evening, Annie had seen JohnJoe gaping at her across the crowded room. She had been casting furtive glances at the good-looking lad since the course had begun. Now she lowered her gaze and hoped he hadn't seen her blushing.

At the local GAA field some wolfish and sex-starved young men attended every camogie match in the hope a gym slip might flare and give them a glimpse of thigh. But JohnJoe wasn't wolfish, and besides, he was only interested in one particular girl. Even though he was inclined to be shy, he drew on what reserves of daring he possessed and walked away from his friends. Soon he "accidentally" encountered Annie Hayes, who was standing alone on the sidelines watching the game through her round-lensed, metal-framed glasses and holding a notebook and a pencil.

I can imagine JohnJoe said something romantic like, "What's wrong wich ya? Why aren't ya out on the playing field?"

Annie would have told him that without her glasses she couldn't see the camogie ball.

"So that's why you're secretary of the club?"

"Yes, and I hear you're a big shot on the selection committee for the county minor hurling team."

"I used to be."

"Oh?"

"Last Monday I proposed Paddy Ruschitzko for the team, but the chairman didn't even look at me. 'I can't spell that name,' he said. Then he shouted, 'Next!' I said I'd spell it for him but he ignored me and called out 'Next!' again. I went up to the table and shouted, 'Is it that you're as thick as a double ditch that you can't spell? Or is it that you're saving a place on the team for your two-ton son who wouldn't know one end of a hurley from the other?' Then I went home."

Annie would not have known then that she had just heard John-Joe's method of dealing with people he considered unfair: assault them with anger and forever after not speak to them because he lacked the tools to rebuild the bridge he had blown up. JohnJoe and Annie would be married and have a child before she realized that in confrontational situations, her husband behaved like a blind man striking out at a biting dog with his stick, hitting himself on the shins and knees as often as he hit the dog.

When the camogie match ended, JohnJoe invited Annie to go with him to the Rock of Dunamaise on the following Sunday. As the blood rushed to her face, Annie managed to croak out, "I'll go if I can borrow a bicycle. I'll let you know Sunday after the eight o'clock mass."

A few days later, when Annie saw JohnJoe in the crowded churchyard, she shook her head, then turned to go home. JohnJoe quick-stepped after her, and when he touched her elbow, she whispered, "People will see us."

"Could you not get a bike?" he asked.

"No."

"Then I'll carry you on the bar of my bike."

"No. If people see me on the bar of your bike they'll think we're—"

"We're what?"

JohnJoe hoped Annie would say "courting." It would establish an understanding between them.

"You know—"

JohnJoe quickly said, "I'll meet you at the Level Crossing with an extra bike at eleven."

"But people will see us and talk."

"When I give you the bike you can head around by the railway bridge, and I'll ride back through the town. I'll be waiting at Carn Bridge."

"But if we meet someone on the way, they'll tell everyone we're hedging and ditching."

This was in an era of church- and society-enforced chastity, when the only place a young couple might be alone was in the countryside under a hedge or in a dry ditch. The local priest had recently declared from the pulpit, "There's too much hedging and ditching in this parish, so I'll be out with me blackthorn stick every night from now on."

JohnJoe reassured Annie of his pure intentions. "Sure, someone would have to see us in a hedge or a ditch first. We'll be on our bikes."

She finally agreed to go.

A half mile north of the railway crossing, Annie's home in the townland of Derrycloney was two miles from JohnJoe's. There, in a three-roomed, thatched cottage she lived with her six siblings and her parents, Martha and Tom. Tom Hayes was a cantankerous fellow who drank most of his wages and demanded his wife boil a brown egg for his breakfast each day. Only a brown egg would suit. What he didn't know was that Martha often served him a white egg that she'd boiled in leftover tea.

Most days when Tom came home from a day of turning barley in Codd's storage building, he was either nasty in his drunkenness or nasty in his craving. Once, after drinking bad poteen, he staggered into the house wielding a pitchfork. Sixteen-year-old Annie tackled him, knocked him to the floor, and twisted the weapon out of his hands.

Despite the poverty of the Hayes cottage, Annie attended the girls' secondary school in Mountmellick. Perhaps some nun in the National School had recommended her and she'd been taken on as a charity case. But she only spent two years in the groves of academe.

"Here comes the scholar," Tom Hayes would jeer. "The scholar reads books while her father kills himself working. . . . Silence in the house when the scholar walks in!" Defeated by her father's constant belittling, Annie left school.

In June 1936, ten months after their meeting at the camogie match, Annie and JohnJoe were married at the 7:30 a.m. mass in the Mountmellick parish church.

In my parents' wedding photo, the youthful JohnJoe's wry smile betrays his discomfort at being out of his farming clothes. Pretty Annie is smiling, her skirt and coat at her calves, her brimmed hat at an angle.

The reception was held in Derrycloney in the front garden of the Hayes cottage, where one of Annie's brothers, my uncle Paulie, took his first sip of alcohol and began the ruination of his life.

As a wedding present JohnJoe gave his bride a red ten-shilling note. He and Annie spent their two-day honeymoon in the Clarence Hotel in Dublin, and Annie ventured forth into the intimidating city to buy clothes for her sisters and brothers. While he waited for her near the shops, JohnJoe leaned over the wall of the River Liffey, watching the boats on the water below. In that position, no smart aleck visiting the city from Mountmellick would notice his choking shirt collar or his tie and tiepin and pass embarrassing remarks:

"Did ya stay up all night, JohnJoe?"

"Keep yer boots on fer a bye, JohnJoe; socks for a gerl."

When the honeymoon was over, Annie took up residence on JohnJoe's farm in Laragh. Forever after, she savored the remembrance of her extraction from Derrycloney and her arrival in her new house with its seven rooms, including a parlor with a wooden floor.

3

THE JUBILEE NURSE

Nurse Byrne was the sparrow that killed Cock Robin with her bow and arrow. Hiding in the elderberry bush near the Harbour Master's house on the Canal Line, her quiver slung across her back, she let fly and sank an arrow into the chest of the bully who thought he was cock of the walk. Little grey and red feathers flew up in the air and floated across the canal like the tiny sails of tiny ships.

In my childish mind, Nurse Byrne and that bushwhacking sparrow were one; the robin was every bully. Birdlike in her shape, eyes, and movements, Nurse Byrne was a tightly wound package of energy. Even at mass on Sundays she was never seen dressed in anything except the feathers of the Jubilee Nurse—navy blue stockings, dress, cardigan, overcoat, and hat. Her gloves and shoes were black.

Nurse Byrne concocted an ointment called Nurse Byrne's Cream. P. J. Walsh, MPSI, sold it in his chemist's shop in round cardboard tubs with her name on the lid. Whenever I heard about a fly in the ointment, I thought the fly was stuck in Nurse Byrne's tub of cream sitting ever ready on the high mantelpiece in our kitchen. Dad rubbed the ointment on cows' dugs when they were sore. He used it, too, to take the squeak out of the wheels of the winter hay cart. When I got ringworm on my face, the ointment was rubbed on every day, and a "special" medal from the nuns was held against my face, too. Later, Mam told the nuns that the medal had worked a miracle.

Nurse Byrne darted beak-first into other people's misfortunes. "Open the door, Mister, and if your wife has any marks on her I'll get Long Tom down here in two shakes." Guard Thomas McGoldrick was called Long Tom to distinguish him from Guard Oliver McGoldrick, who was called Spuds. Dad said Spuds carried a bag of potatoes in the seat of his trousers.

Nurse Byrne washed the dead with Lifebuoy soap and blocked their orifices with wads of cotton wool. She dressed the corpses in their shrouds and positioned them in their beds in preparation for their waking. Except in Protestant houses, she weaved a set of rosary beads through the cold fingers and clamped the dead hands together in an attitude of prayerful humility for eternity. "And don't light a fire in the wake room."

She spent a lot of her time on her bike wobbling around deep potholes in mucky country lanes in Mountmellick's environs. Much of her life was spent in kitchens rubbing ointment on children with various ailments. Sometimes she dosed a child like Dad dosing a sick cow out of a long-necked bottle, the cow's head pulled to one side and up, the eyes bulging—Dad's two fingers up the cow's nostrils to hold the head steady. Even though tears ran down the child's face and he tried to wiggle away, Nurse Byrne always won because of the fierceness of her eyes and the sharpness of her bird tongue and the strength of her tiny wings, and the medicine went into the mouth and down the throat without a drop spilled. "Now, that wasn't too bad, was it, child? You'll be better before you can say Jack Robinson."

For noisy chests and suppurating wounds and boils, she made poultices from a mixture of hot bran and goose grease. Goose grease was also rubbed into sprained ankles before they were tightly bound in bandages cut from white flour sacks. She used guilt and guile on farmers to give her dry bran and goose grease for poorer families. Out of her own pocket, she bought jars of sweet and gooey Mount-mellick Malt and brought them to houses where the children were not thriving. "Now, that's not for spreading on bread. It's for the children; one spoon each in the morning and before bed."

She stood up to big men, fluttering her wings while she pecked at them for abusing their wives and children with their porter drinking. "There's no bigger eejit than a drunk father; hanging is too good for you, Mister. Shame on you! Shame on you!"

She had the same respect for the poor and not-poor, and if a tongue-lashing was deserved, then it was fearlessly delivered. She shouted at Father Kelly in public for allowing his dog to run free and knock Missus Fitz off her bike and break her hip, reduced him by her form of address: "If you can't control your dog, *Mister* Kelly, then don't keep a dog. You have no respect for other people."

The nurse dressed the ulcerated legs of women who had borne too many children. She changed bandages for farmers who injured themselves with machinery. She cut fishhooks out of eyebrows and lips. She sewed up scrotums that had been ripped on the barbs of barbed wire.

"Ah, Nurse, shure I'm too shy to show ya me bag."

"Mister," she'd reply, with hands on hips, "you don't have a bag; you have a scrotum, and I see scrotums hanging out of dogs and bulls and asses and horses every day. There's nothing special about yours. Take off your trousers and stop thinking your scrotum is any better than a stray dog's."

She dressed wounds caused by flesh-ripping saws, finger-squashing hammers, bone-piercing chisels, through-the-foot crowbars, awk-wardly swung mallets, through-the-hand awls, cutting-to-the-bone fishing lines, stepped-on glass, drunken falls from bikes, hand-squashing iron-shod cart wheels, flesh-eating drums of turnip pulpers, piercing slivers of wood from the blades of wielded hatchets, and stepped-on rusty nails, which required the administration of an injection.

"Be a man, for God's sake! It's only a needle. Try giving birth to a baby someday and you'll know what pain is."

She repaired those who'd been kicked by horses and gored by horns or who had done a bad job of trying to kill themselves. "If you don't come to see me before you try this again, I won't lay you out for your wake and you'll lie there in the bed all crooked with your eyes bulging and your tongue hanging out, and your water leaking out of you and stinking, and won't that be a grand sight for your mother and father!"

Like Dad pulling calves out of cows, Nurse Byrne pulled three generations of babies out of their mothers in Mountmellick and its surrounding townlands. To some houses she brought her own towels and only demanded warm water. When she delivered me and slapped my bottom I cried so loudly that she muttered, "This lad has a voice that would fill a church."

Those were the first words spoken about me *ex utero*. Because it was the Jubilee Nurse who uttered them, the Oracle at Delphi had spoken. I imprinted on the church like a chicken imprinting on the duck that has accidentally hatched it out. The course of my life was set before the slime and blood of birth had even been cleaned off me. The nurse's words became so firmly attached to me that four years later, on my first day in school, I was told by three nuns that I would make a lovely priest. Pious believers had taken the midwife's words and run before me, preparing my way and making straight the highway to the priesthood.

As she grew older Nurse Byrne's hearing began to fail.

"Will you stop whispering for God's sake? What's the matter with you?"

She spoke louder, repeated herself more often. Whenever she passed me on her bike in the town she screeched, "When you were born you had the loudest cry I ever heard, Tom Phelan, and the biggest b-o-t-tom, too." And she rode on, leaving me at the mercy of the lads who had heard her. "Big Arse Phelan! Big Arse!"

Near the end of her days, Nurse Byrne bought a car and became the terror of the town's children and dogs. She had grown so small that she only saw a slice of the world between the dashboard and the rim of the steering wheel.

When she died, it was as if a mountain had been moved off the horizon during the night. The Cock Robins of the town once again swaggered in the domain that had been hers for forty-odd years. Most of the babies she had pulled out were at her funeral.

It wasn't until her headstone was put up that the town discovered that Nurse Byrne's name was Katherine.

4

IN THE FARMHOUSE KITCHEN

In our farmhouse on Laragh Lane in Mountmellick, the kitchen was also the dining room, the children's playroom, the sitting room, the workroom, the place where turkeys and chickens were plucked, and where new litters of pigs were kept warm in cardboard boxes while Dad broke off their front teeth with pliers to prevent them from biting their mother's teats.

The only source of heat in the house was the kitchen fireplace. The bedrooms and parlor were cold and damp, and we slept with our school clothes folded between the sheets to have them warm for the following morning. Hot water bottles were used for most of the year. All dry overcoats in the house served as extra blankets.

On Saturday nights in our kitchen, preparations were made for attendance at mass the next morning: Dad shaved, Mam polished shoes, Dad washed the children, Mam dried us and fine-combed our hair for fleas, and Dad trimmed our nails.

· Early in the evening the big black cast-iron pot—also used for boiling gruel, potatoes for the pigs, Christmas puddings, and Monday-morning laundry water—was hung from the crane above

the fire. Because the hard limestone water from the well made it difficult to work up a lather, the pot was filled with soft water from the
concrete tank at the wicket door.

"But I saw worms wriggling in the tank."

"Sure, what's a few boiled worms?"

While the water heated, Mam placed a basin, towel, shaving
brush, yellow soap, comb, and folded newspaper on the table in
preparation for Dad's weekly performance with his razor. Then she
sat at the fire, with her back to the place of Dad's high-wire act, and
shined the shoes. As if the smell of Kiwi polish activated an alarm in
his brain, Dad stood up and walked into the boys' room. He returned
with the wood-framed, tilting, shaving mirror.

The money box on top of the dresser was never touched by the
children; neither was the Sacred Heart lamp, the key to the kitchen
door, the serrated bread knife, Mam's rod hanging beneath the mantelpiece, the door latch of Uncle Jack's room, the sugar bowl, the
matches on the mantel, or the key for winding the clock. But above
all else, Dad's razor was so much off-limits that I imagined it was a
murderous weapon with a mind of its own, ever watchful for flesh as
it lay in its lair in the drawer under the mirror. It was a wild animal
that only the strong hand of a man could control, but even in the
strongest of hands, it could still sink its teeth into the face of the
shaver.

When Dad lifted the paraffin lamp off its nail on the wall and
placed it beside the mirror, the shadows in the kitchen changed, rob-
bing it of its familiar, comforting qualities. The atmosphere became
colder, and the anticipation of Dad's derring-do caused the hairs on
my neck to move.

My four siblings and I gaped at Dad shaving as if mesmerized
by a snake's twitching tongue. Down the side of his face the razor
loudly scraped, leaving in its wake a clean, pink swath. I held my face
within my palms as Dad's cheeks and jaws appeared from under the
soap.

I had often helped Dad as he slit the throats of turkeys bound for the Christmas market, and so I grasped the seat of my chair when he dragged his razor down his throat, not even slowing as it approached his Adam's apple, and bumped over it like a bike going over Rourke's Bridge. Then the razor was climbing back up his throat to clear the stubbles the downward passes had missed. The slopes of his Adam's apple were ascended and descended with no regard for safety. With thumb and index finger at each side of my throat, I pressed against my skin to save him from slicing into a pulsing artery. More soap was brushed on and the fingers of Dad's left hand were used to make level the passage of the razor across the hilly surfaces of his chin. When he lifted his nose to get at his philtrum, exposing his nostrils in the mirror, my sister put her hands over her eyes and bent her head to the table.

"He looks like a pig," she said.

When Dad finally finished, he hung the lamp back on its nail, and the familiar comfort and warmth of the kitchen returned.

Back at the basin, Dad lathered his hands. Then, like a starling in a loch of water on Laragh Lane, he scrubbed his face and ears and neck, his face almost in the basin, drops of water in the air around him. Then he scooped water over his head, and washed his hair with the yellow soap. When he'd rinsed out most of it, he poked his ears with his thick farmer's fingers.

"Nan," he said, and Mam dipped a saucepan into the pig pot, cooling it with mugs of cold water from the kitchen bucket. She held the pan over Dad's head, the soapy water falling into the basin like liquid icicles pouring off the eaves of a thatched roof on a long day of heavy rain. Then Dad toweled himself with the same intensity he applied to everything he did: his head became the center of a flurry, a whirlwind towel chased by two hands full of impatient fingers.

Next he ran a close-toothed, flea-catching, ivory comb through his soft hair, inspecting it for victims after each pass. If he found one he squashed it between his thumbnail and the ivory, the tinny click bringing a protesting grunt from my sister. Then before resuming the hunt he wiped the comb on the arse of his trousers.

When he had stowed away the mirror and cleared the table, Dad put on his cap and went out to the dairy to fetch the two-handled galvanized bath. The bath was also used for the Monday morning laundry and as a carrier for apples and potatoes. Once a year it was positioned beneath a lifeless, hanging pig to catch its intestines when Mister Lowndes slit its belly from nave to chaps with one drag of his knife.

To our boggish tongues the bath was a "baa." It was three feet long with fifteen-inch sides, a handle at each end. Giving loud instructions for everyone to stand back, Dad lifted the pig pot off its hook over the fire, carried it to the baa in the middle of the floor and, using his cap to grasp one of the three legs, tilted in most of the water. Steam billowed to the clothesline near the ceiling.

Soon Dad was on the floor beside the baa, roughly scrubbing a child's body.

"Ow!"

"Well, if you didn't get your insteps so dirty . . ."

When my turn came and the stinging soap was rubbed into my hair, I clamped my eyes shut until the saucepan delivered its cascade of flushing water. Then I stepped out of the baa into the towel on Mam's lap at the fireplace. When she had dried me, brushed my hair straight, and used the ivory flea-catcher, I was unseated to make room for the next child. Those few moments in her lap within the radius of the fire's heat were like soaking in a bath of warm, silver grace.

In pajamas and shoes we lined up to have our nails cut. Using scissors large enough to trim a box hedge, Dad examined each finger for signs of nail biting. When an accusation was made and a lie of denial told, the accused received a slap on the back of the hand; the evidence of biting was pointed to, the accusation was repeated, and the truth was told.

"You'll have to tell that lie in confession."

Our Saturday night ablutions completed, Mam and Dad lifted the bathful of used water onto two chairs facing each other "to get it out of the way," and then we were sent to bed, hot water bottles under our oxters.

Years later I realized Mam had bathed in the baa water after we children had gone to sleep.

5

THE TURKEY IN
THE CUPBOARD

Our kitchen dresser had three shelves atop a wider cupboard with two doors. The lower two shelves held the everyday delft, and the top one displayed three Willow pattern serving dishes with hairline cracks in the glaze exposing the brown clay beneath. Along the dresser's crown, a row of chipped mugs and cups holding small bits and pieces, saved "just in case," hung on hooks. A tin cigar box on top of the dresser held the petty cash and important papers like dog and bull licenses; up there, too, were catapults taken from misbehaving boys.

Mam used the surface of the cupboard below the shelves as her workbench. Inside the cupboard she stored the bread baker, pots, saucepans, frying pan, and a sack of flour. Every spring she tidied these to one side and made a nest of soft barley straw in the empty space. When one of her turkey hens sat down in the middle of the farmyard in a state of broodiness and refused to move, Mam gathered her up, placed her on the nest, and closed the cupboard door.

The next morning Mam left the cupboard open until the turkey came out. The bird was calmly steered to the kitchen door, where she tripped over the shallow step. The moment she entered the graveled yard, one of the children chased her to the dunghill in the haggard. There the turkey stood, pointed her tail to the sky, and sent out a blast of turd that landed ten feet away, leaving a contrail of stinky steam. After she had adjusted her feathers, she was driven back into the farmyard. There she was introduced to two battered tin saucepans, one filled with water, the other with a mash of crushed oats, chopped hardboiled eggs, potatoes, and dandelions.

She ate in solitude, but because memories of gang-feeding with her siblings when she was a chick were etched into the turkey's brain, she gobbled up her mash as if making sure she would be the one fittest to survive. Then she stuck her beak in the water, trapped a drop, and lifted her beak to the sky to let the water flow down her gullet. She did everything quickly, Uncle Jack said, because she couldn't stop thinking about her nest.

Full to her wattles, she trotted back to the kitchen door, cocked her head, and listened. When she heard nothing, she nervously stepped in, fell down the two-inch step, jerked her head, and blinked her purple eyelids. She walked over to the dresser, all the while scoping out the kitchen for a predator waiting to pounce. Then she poked her head into the nest, which now contained fourteen brown-speckled white eggs. Mam had bought the eggs from Alice Burns, whose boar regularly impregnated Dad's sows. Turkey cocks can be vicious and dangerous to children, so Mam did not keep one when we were small.

Without hesitating to ponder the miraculous appearance of the clutch of eggs, she straddled the nest, sat down carefully, and fussed until every egg was under her feathers. Mam, who had been sitting still at the end of the dresser, quietly closed the door, and everyone in the kitchen moved again.

Each morning for the next twenty-eight days, when it was time for the hatching turkey to go out, everyone in the kitchen played statues. When she came off her nest, she stood still as a stick on the cold kitchen floor. Then, when she saw it was safe, she walked to the kitchen door, stumbled over the shallow step, and strode out into the farmyard. One of the children immediately chased her to the haggard, the bird running like a person with their arms tied to the sides of their body.

Turkeys normally do their jow countless times a day wherever they happen to be. But a clocking turkey makes her jow once a day, when she comes off her nest. So every morning in the kitchen, there were complaints about driving the turkey out to the haggard.

"Why do I always have to see her stinky dung squarting? Ask Eddie to do it."

"I fed the ferret last night and his dung is stinkier than the turkey's."

One time when I steered the turkey out to the dunghill, Dad and Uncle Jack were working in the haggard. The bird let fly a squart with a trail of steam rising off it like smoke off a burning stick.

"That must tear d'arse out of her," Uncle Jack said.

"The child, Jack!" Dad said, nodding toward me.

Once, the turkey thought she saw a fox in a dark kitchen corner, and in her fright she flew up toward the light in the window. She bumped into the glass and fell onto her back, her claws entangled in the lace curtain. Hanging upside down with her wings fluttering, she sent everything stored on the wide windowsill scattering onto the floor—caps, pixies, gloves, newspapers, the *Irish Messenger of the Sacred Heart*, a ball of wool with two knitting needles stuck in it. She squawked like she was being murdered. Mam folded the wings against the turkey's body and calmed her down by putting the head in her armpit. Then she told my sister to untangle the curtain from the turkey's claws; in dread of touching the scaly feet and sharp nails, she obeyed with a squinched-up face and nervous fingers, whining, "Why do I always have to do it?"

Fortunately, this happened when the turkey was on the way back from her daily toilette.

During the third week of hatching, Mam put the eggs in a basin of warm water she had tested with her elbow. If an egg floated it was fertile; if it sank it was rotting, and my brothers and I fought for the joy of splattering it against the cow house in a shower of dark yellow stink.

When the eggs in the dresser hatched out, Mam took the tiny birds out to the turkey house in a bucket. There she fed them her special mash of chopped nettle and dandelion, egg, medicated powder, bran, bone meal, and bread until they were big enough to be steered out to the Limekiln Field to graze and scratch.

In late summer, when the sheaves of wheat, barley, and oats had been drawn into the haggard, one of my jobs was to herd the flock of turkeys to one of the fields so they could glean the kernels that had fallen out during the cutting and handling of the cereal. For a couple of hours, they high-stepped through the short, hard stubbles like a man high-stepping through dewy grass in a pair of leaky wellingtons.

When I drove the turkeys home to the farmyard, Mam came out and helped me count the ever-moving, tightly packed flock. If our counts did not agree, we did it again.

Precautions, similar to making a kitchen childproof, were taken against the myriad ways the turkeys could accidentally kill themselves. Mam said, "Turkeys are so stupid they can drown by standing in the rain and looking up at the sky with their beaks open." The calves' water tank in the Limekiln Field was a great attraction for the birds. But when they flew up onto the rim, they lost their balance, toppled in, and went to a watery grave. Even after Dad placed a partial lid on the tank, some turkeys still managed to drown themselves. And on occasion Old Mister Fox greased his chin with turkey flesh until Dad caught him in a snare.

Each year, Mam reared about eighty turkeys for the Christmas market and to give as gifts. The birds she sold produced a little wave of money that would float our holiday extravagances, such as a bag of coal for the fireplace and a toy for each child. The parish priest and the nuns in Mountmellick, Granny, our aunt Teresa in Dublin, our aunt Kit in England, and several others received turkeys, while friends and men who had worked with Dad during the year got a pair of chickens or a duck.

Each December, Dad and his helpers gathered the birds not destined to be gifts, tied their legs together, loaded them into the horse's cart, and brought them to the market in the town square. About ten days before Christmas, Dad killed all the gift turkeys. First, he folded the wings and put the bird between his knees. One year, when I was about ten, I was assigned to hold the bird's legs projecting behind Dad to keep them still. Dad grasped the turkey's head, bent up the neck, and cut across it with the broken kitchen knife he had sharpened on the wall of the sandstone trough. The pain and struggles of the bird went into its legs and then up my arms and into my chest. Later, when I asked Dad not to ask me to do that job anymore, I was surprised when he said yes; I had been afraid he would tell me to be a man.

When the turkeys had experienced the one bad day in their otherwise happy lives, they were hung upside down on iron spikes high in the dairy walls. During the week they were there, it was only my fear of disobeying Dad that forced me into the dairy, my half-hooded eyes avoiding the slit throats and purple heads.

The turkeys were plucked at night in the pallid yellow light of the double-wicked paraffin-oil lamp hanging on the whitewashed kitchen wall. Dad and Mam and Uncle Jack plucked, each sitting on a straight-backed kitchen chair, each with a soft beet-pulp sack across their knees and a dead bird in their lap, the head hanging down and almost touching the floor, eyes closed. The sound of the feathers being ripped out was like the sound of a piece of paper being torn from top to bottom. Sometimes one of the pluckers made a *tsk*, meaning they had scarred the bird's skin.

The pluckers always left the wing feathers on because the person getting the turkey might dry the wings to use them to sweep crumbs of turf and ashes into the ash pit.

Once, while plucking, shy Uncle Jack said out of the blue, "Gussie McFlynn rode a hin from here to Ballyfin. When he came back, he made a crack and blew the feathers off her back."

As the adults worked, movement in the kitchen was restricted because the breezy wakes of passing children swirled the plucked feathers up into the air, causing them to be breathed into nostrils and set off sneezing fits. And when a feather landed on the open fire, it hissed and made a foul smell like hair burning. Sometimes the flames of the oil lamp on the wall leaped up and devoured a feather that had floated across the top of its glass globe.

Dad was the one who pulled out the pinfeathers of all the birds with pliers. He was the one who tied the feet of the naked birds together and hung them upside down again on the nails in the walls in the dairy. He also kept Mam and Uncle Jack supplied with dead birds. Dad was a great organizer. Mam once said, "If the Irish army marched into our farmyard, Dad would assign a job to each soldier as he passed by."

On the morning after the plucking, all the feathers were gone from the kitchen. Mam spent the day preparing the turkeys that would go to the Post Office. She did not cut off the feet, wings, or head, nor did she draw them. "They travel better with their guts in," she said. Mam folded the wings, the neck, and the feet against the body and tied them with white twine. She weighed the bird on the spring scales hanging on the wall, said a number to herself, and wrote it on a label. Next, she wrapped the bird in butter paper and tied it in place with twine; she did the same with a sheet of brown paper; then, with needle and thread, she sewed the whole thing into a piece of an Odlum's flour sack. The turkey looked like a lumpy football in a tight sock with its end sewed up. "That's the way the Post Office says to do it," Mam said. Then she wrote an address and the weight of the contents on the label.

When Mam had all the turkeys ready, Dad caught the black pony, yoked her to the trap, and carried out the parcels. Turkey season was over for Mam, except for preparing a bird for our Christmas dinner. On Christmas morning, she spread live turf coals on the hearth, placed the lidded cast-iron baker holding the turkey on them, and then surrounded the baker with more glowing coals.

Our beautiful brown Christmas turkey marked the high point of our culinary year.

LOVE WRIT SHYLY

Dad, with his all-devouring work ethic, was a large presence in my young life. Mam was the sheltering harbor from the storms that sometimes raged in Dad's head and spewed out in loud and angry words.

But Mam never became the object of Dad's anger. He loved and respected her. Although I never heard either of my parents express words of affection to each other, Dad showed his love for Mam in many small and silent ways. Later in life, I came to understand that his attentiveness to her was love writ shyly.

Dad was always taking care of Mam. Before going to the fields, he renewed the freshwater bucket in the kitchen and filled the turf box. He washed the potatoes for the midday meal; he picked cabbage from the garden and cleaned it; he cut pieces off the preserved side of bacon. He did all the farmyard chores, including churning the milk, and when we children grew big, he delegated those jobs to us. On Saturday nights, he was half the team that washed and scrubbed the bodies of the children and inspected their hair for living creatures.

Besides rearing turkeys for the Christmas market, Mam did farm work only in an emergency. Even though she had milked the family cow when she was a child in Derrycloney, Dad did not allow her to do this; in his mind, a milking woman was married to a lazy and thoughtless man.

Every morning, Mam prepared breakfast for the family, as well as for whoever had come to work for Dad. When the men were toiling in the fields, she brought tea to them at eleven and four, along with slices of her homemade currant cake. If the farm work was being rushed to keep ahead of looming rain, Mam carried entire dinners of bacon, cabbage, spuds, tea, and cake out to the men at one o'clock. Then at six, she fed all the workers in the kitchen before they headed home. On threshing days, with neighborly assistance, she cooked for a couple dozen men.

I don't remember Mam ever sitting at the table with us while we ate, not even on Christmas Day. When everyone else's needs were tended to, she sat at the fire with her plate in her lap. Perhaps this made it easier to serve any needs that cropped up at the table; perhaps her family had not eaten together when she was growing up in Derrycloney; perhaps she was taking a break from us children. As a result, Dad was the one who instructed us in basic table manners. But his lessons were not motivated by concern for our dining etiquette; he was teaching us the safe use of eating utensils.

"Don't ever put your knife in your mouth; if you do, you might cut your lips. Or your tongue."

"Don't point at anyone with a knife or fork; you might poke their eye out."

Dad's lifelong closeness to the earth and animals had inured him to things an average person would balk at. He inserted his whole arm into cows to move misaligned calves onto the proper track for birthing; he handled afterbirth; he broke newborn pigs' milk teeth with pliers; he squashed flocks of cabbage-eating green caterpillars between his fingers; he paunched, skinned, and otherwise prepared rabbits for the dinner pot; he burned the incipient horns off young calves with a stick of caustic soda; he held turkeys and chickens between his thighs, bent up their necks, and cut their throats; he stuck his forefinger and thumb into the nostrils of cattle to immobilize them; he whacked aging hens on the back of their heads with a knobby stick to put them out of their misery; he castrated young bulls and pigs; he once castrated a young stallion with a cut-throat razor; he lopped the tails off pups; he crawled along drills to thin out sugar beet seedlings and encountered every kind of slimy creepy-crawly with his bare hands; he taught us how to impale wiggling worms on barbarous fishhooks.

Yet when it came to eating, Dad was easily put off by the sight of anything that reminded him of the farmyard. Runny eggs were never served in his presence; the flowing yolk looked too much like something too disgusting to mention; macaroni was also reminiscent of something too disgusting to mention; the smell of onions, raw or cooked, was that of horse farts. Slurping at the table was forbidden, not just because it was impolite, but also because it reminded Dad of a hairy-faced sow, jaw-deep in its slop; a child's open, food-filled mouth was like the rear of a cow at a moment too disgusting to mention; loud chewing noises were rats gnawing turnips; food around the mouth was that hairy-faced sow again; banging plates with a knife or fork was Peetie Flanagan in his forge that stunk of anthracite and equine emanations.

Dad's own table manners were those of a country person who had never been burdened with the choices presented at a formal dining table. One knife, one fork, and one spoon were sufficient unto whatever was served. At the kitchen table, when he was poured a cup of tea, he sugared it, milked it, stirred it, and poured a third of it into his saucer. Then he picked up the saucer with one hand and drank. When the saucer was empty, he put it back on the table, placed his cup on it, and drank the rest of his tea from the cup. When we children asked Dad why he did this, he meowed.

In the days following Christmas, Mam served turkey at dinnertime until the bird's bones were bare. But because Dad could not tolerate waste, the carcass was put on his plate for one last picking. As I silently recited grace, my eyes were drawn to the remains of the turkey, looking like the ribs of a rotten ship floating in a tiny lake.

Dad raised the skeleton to his mouth and tore off small pieces of flesh. He poked in bony corners with his two-pronged, buck-handled knife. Many times, his face was completely hidden by the ribs as he hunted for more evasive morsels; he sucked at them until he caught them between his teeth. He held the rear end of the skeleton to his eye and peeped out through the hole at the other end where the neck had once been anchored.

He was a sailor on the deck of a ship, looking through a glass. As he pointed the telescope from child to child, he said, "Whale ahoy! And I see a yack on the horizon."

My brothers and I laughed and begged, "Do it again!"

But my sister said, "It's a yacht! Not a yack!" in a tone to show she was not amused.

Next, with crackings and snappings, Dad broke the ribs off the backbone. He examined each bone, and if bearing any prize, subjected it to sucking lips and reaching teeth. A few times, he pretended to play the mouth organ on a bone, humming and acting out a tremolo with his right hand while peeping through his eyelashes at us children. Around his plate, the cleaned bones piled up until there was nothing left in his hands but the notched backbone. This piece took a long time to be rendered meatless, as every nook and cranny was explored with fingers, fork, and tongue. When it finally found its place on the pile of debris, Dad said to my sister, "I'm finished. You can put the turkey back together now." We all laughed, except Dad. I never once heard him give a loud or hearty laugh.

Mam removed the ossuary and threw it in the fire. Dad asked, "Tom, what's that saying about the crows and food?"

"If you throw food away, you'll follow the crows for it over the mountain."

"All those scraps of meat came from Mam's hard work with the turkeys. Never waste your mother's labor."

As the acrid smell of the burning bones filled the kitchen, Mam gave Dad a rag and he wiped the grease off his face.

Every day, Dad organized the cleaning up after dinner, with himself doing the washing. We children dried the dishes, put them away, and swept the concrete floor. As we worked, Mam sat at the fire, reading the death notices on the front page of the *Irish Independent* or about the royal family in *Woman's Weekly*. It was another little act of love by Dad.

MY FIFTY-TWO-ACRE
PLAYGROUND

From the time we grew out of our nappies, the fifty-two acres of Dad's farm were our playground. My brothers and sisters and I knew every dip and rise in the fields, where a nest of cowslips grew, where the first primroses sent forth their perfume. We knew the floral residents of every hedge, where a bunch of purple violets came back every year, where hazelnuts turned brown and fell from their cups, where honeysuckle made its tempting but poisonous berries, where crab apple trees waited for the first frost to turn their bitter fruit sweet, where wild gooseberry bushes hid among the fierce protection of the blackthorns.

All the dividing hedges in the fields grew out of banks of earth, and it was here we checked for rabbit burrows and badger setts and fox dens, examining the entrances for fresh tracks. We knew all the hedge gaps we could creep through without fear of jabbing thorn, stinging nettle, or barbed wire.

We visited the birds' nests we had seen being built, and lifted each other up to look at the eggs or the newly hatched scalds. We could touch the eggs if our fingers were wet with spit, and it was permissible to take one egg; the bird would not miss it.

In the summer, when fresh bovine plops were plentiful, the yellow, translucent dung flies feasted. "Look out!" one brother would shout, as his ashplant whizzed through the air and split the dung, sent it flying, and killed the flies. And then, in imitation of the SOS messages broadcast on Radio Eireann, another brother would announce: *Will Mister Christopher Fly, last heard of in Manchester thirty-five years ago, please call the garda barracks in Clonaslee for an important message about his cowplop cousins?*

On Sundays we always went "across the fields" to play, but also to escape from Dad. Sunday or not, he could not tolerate idleness in adult or child. We never got lost but, if we had, we would easily have found our bearings by looking for Joe Mack's Tree and the church spire in the town.

One summer Sunday when my brother Eddie and I were sneaking silently around the field hedges with our pellet guns, looking for small birds to shoot, we ended up at the Beech Trees. The trees were close to a lane that ran along the bank of the canal. When we heard someone yelling, "Will yiz stop yer talking and frightnen the fishes!" we peeped through the leafy hedge and saw a group of men and boys from the town scattered along the far Canal Bank, all fishing for roach. We knew they were fishing for roach because in front of each fisherman a cork was sitting in the water. The corks, which had been scrounged out of the local pubs, kept the roach bait off the bottom of the canal. The bait consisted of flour mixed with water and strands of sheep wool to keep it on the hook, and the fishing poles were all homemade, created from hazel striplings.

Soon, Eddie and I decided we'd climb up into one of the Beech Trees and shoot pellets at the fishermen's corks. As quiet as stalking cats, we settled ourselves behind a screen of leafy branches. We fired and a pellet sent up a spurt of water near a floating cork.

"Didja see dat?" a man roared.

"I heard a shot!" another yelled.

We let off another salvo.

"Someone's shooting out of dem trees!" a man shouted. Then he dropped his fishing pole and ran toward the bridge that would take him across to our side.

"Get deh cur!" another man cried and he, too, headed to the bridge.

Terrified, Eddie and I scrambled down out of the tree and ran with our guns across the Rushes into the field at Frank's Lane. Down Joe Mack's Lane we galloped, the fear of being murdered urging us on. Out into Frank's Big Field we clamored through the strands of barbed wire, but before we got to the far side, the fishermen were coming over the fence in the same place.

Over the gate into Frank's Pasture we vaulted and out onto the cart track running down past the Crutcheen, the Back Batens, and out into the Long Field. Tears of fear were blinding me. We were deep into the countryside now, half a mile from the nearest house. But we were so winded that we couldn't go any farther. We quickly hid our guns under the dry weeds growing across a drain. Then we lay down in the grass to await our fate.

The two men came upon us. "Where's the guns?"

"What guns?" we asked, our voices wobbling.

"We know you lads are Phelans. . . . Your father will be hearing about this!"

"About what?" I asked, shakily getting to my feet.

"You eejits! We know you were shooting at us. A pellet could bounce off the water, go into someone's eye, and blind them." They were so angry I was afraid they might knock us unconscious with a knuckled fist under the chin like in the cowboy pictures. Or maybe they'd hang us.

"Why did you run away from us?"

"We didn't run away from you."

"Why are you breathing like that then?"

"We just ran from that hedge down there up to here when we saw them two lads running across the field." I pointed. My voice was still hobbling along on a rubber crutch.

They looked across the field. They looked at each other.

"You're a liar."

"No, I'm not."

We were asked to describe the two boys we had seen.

"They were too far away . . . we only saw them for a second before they went through the gap."

"How big were they?"

"About our size."

"What kind of trousers were they wearing?"

"Short, like ours."

"You're a liar."

"No, I'm not."

"Yes, y'are."

"If you do it again we'll kill the two of you."

"Do what?"

"Oh, shag off!"

As they turned to go away, one of them said, "Little feckers!"

At a terrified distance, Eddie and I followed them across the fields until we saw them going back out onto the Canal Line. Then we went back and retrieved our weapons. We took a long way home, around by Joe Mack's Tree.

We must have sowed doubt in the minds of the two fishermen because they never told Dad what we did. I know this for a fact because I am still alive.

8

THE LOVELY CHURCH

The war was blamed for many things; the price of everything had gone up since the war started. Flour wasn't milled properly anymore, and Granny sieved out the impure bits in an old stocking while a fine cloud drifted down to a sheet of newspaper on our kitchen table. The inner tubes of bikes were repaired so often that the patches themselves were patched. Petrol was rationed, Mister Hayden used TVO—Tractor Vaporizing Oil—to run his van, and sparks in showers flew out from the exhaust pipe. Instead of sugar, saccharine pills sat in egg cups on tables, so sweet they burned the tongue when surreptitiously slipped into the mouth. Tobacco was scarce and some people put beet pulp in their pipes. Tea leaves were saved and reused and, when they had no more to give, they were dried and smoked in pipes or in tubes made from newspaper. The smokers coughed like cows with the hoose. The war squeezed the color out of clothes until all that was left were navy blues and browns. Only for the green grass and the blue sky and the flowers of spring and summer, the world was black and white; except in the church—the huge, magnificent, spotless, colorful, musical church built and adorned to house God.

We can never know the utter astonishment our medieval ancestors felt when they approached one of the great cathedrals for the first
time. Our forebears lived in dark, cold, low-roofed, leaking, draughty,
smoky huts. For the well-off, wattle and daub served as walls; tree
branches and grassy clods kept some of the rain out. When the peas-
antry, at the behest of wandering monks, set out on pilgrimages to
cathedrals in Chartres, Salzburg, Paris, York, Cologne, Winchester,
or Lincoln, they walked barefooted along dark and narrow forest
paths. Traveling inside leafy tunnels for weeks, with their faces bent
to the ground, they carefully picked their way over roots and rocks
and holes. Along the way, they ate berries off bushes, drank from
forest streams. When they got lost, they stumbled around in circles
for days until they found the path again. Some got sick and some
died. During the long trip, they must have wondered if the monks
had scammed them, wondered if, while they were plodding off on
the pilgrimage, the monks back home were prodding their wives, as
Rabelais suspected.

Then one day, the pilgrims unexpectedly emerged into a sunlit
clearing and were faced with the most immense, stupendous, most
infinite and massive, most overwhelming and frightening thing they
had ever encountered. They might as well have been prehistoric canoe-
ists on a small lake, suddenly aware the *Titanic* was bearing down on
them. They did not know what it was, but what they were seeing rose
up into the sky where God lived. They weakened at the knees and
dropped to the ground on the spot.

Eventually, when they saw other people approaching this gar-
gantuan edifice, they summoned the strength to stand. Shyly and
fearfully, they sidled up to the massive entrance, exposed their dirty
arses every time they tripped over a step and fell their way up to
the eighteen-foot-high entrance. There in the bronze castings on
the doors were tiny, naked people falling down into leaping flames;
an angel with a flaming sword; a man and woman slinking into a
pile of bushes; a giant's head with a boy holding it up by the hair;

goats, sheep, trees; crowds on knees staring up at a dancing sun; a goat with a man's face standing on its rear hooves and laughing, horns on its head and a long tail; a man pouring water over another man's head.

Stepping on each other's heels like a herd of nervous gnus hearing a rustle in the dry savanna grass, the pilgrims shuffled inside. Their fearful glances swept the length and width and height of the cathedral; the space; the brightness; the size of the pillars; the shapes; the colors and colors and colors. It was angels who had splashed the colors all over.

Heaven had been trapped within the massive structure. It was a miracle, for only God could build a house and have colored light streaming through the walls. And then they saw people and goats and sheep and cows in the colored light. The things God could do!

The walls themselves were higher than the highest fir tree. It was God Himself who had made the enormous, glistening pillars. He had made the towers in heaven and then stuck them down in the ground so that men could climb up and talk to Him, see the edge of the world, see mountains they thought were monstrous blue snails.

• Again their knees gave out; they were in the presence of God in God's own house; they were inside God. They did not, and never would, have the words to tell the village back home what they were seeing. How could they describe the size and the towers and the colors to people living in a tiny forest clearing, people who had never seen a sunrise or a sunset because the trees were so tall, whose hut floors were earthen, with holes large enough to break an ankle in; who did not have "clean" in their vocabulary?

The pilgrims would not have had the words to describe the steady flames or the candles that gave them life, or the richly colored and gold-threaded vestments, the smell of incense, the voices of the choirs echoing off the distant vaults. How could they ever imitate those sounds for the folks back in the woods?

The pilgrims would eventually return home, but they would never be the same again. Some became so dissatisfied with their surroundings that they went back to the cathedral and offered themselves to the service of the magnificent edifice as a doorkeeper, reader, exorcist, acolyte, subdeacon, deacon, or priest. Of course, if they were accepted they would have to throw away their skins, go sit in the nearest river, and scrub themselves with sand for a week. "And cut the talons off your toes! Here's my axe."

I could not claim to have had the same cathedral experience as my ancestors when, in the middle of the Second World War, I first toddled into our local church holding Mam's hand. But over time, everything beautiful and stupendous about the building seeped into my consciousness. With each attendance at Sunday mass I became more aware of the colors; the saints and animals in the stained glass windows; the geometric designs with no beginning or end; the bloodred flame in the filigreed, enormous silver sanctuary lamp hanging from the depths of the ceiling; the brilliant whiteness of the intricately carved marble reredos; the six tall flickering candles in front of them; the polished terrazzo floor; the arches dividing the nave from the side aisles, the marble angels on top of the pillars holding up the arches on their backs; the sky-high brown wooden ceiling looking like it had been knitted into patterns by giant women with giant knitting needles; the lights hanging on ropes that disappeared into the ceiling folds; the gold of the tabernacle door when the small silk curtain was pulled aside; the liturgical colors draped on the altar and embroidered into the priests' vestments; the embossed, golden-threaded symbols all pulling the eye to IHS in its circle; the smell of snuffed candles and billowing incense; the sound of the curved brass gong announcing the Consecration; the red cassocks of the altar boys; the vases of jumbled flowers; the little arches of the altar rails, with their black and green pillars of Connemara marble and the filigreed brass gates allowing access to the sanctuary; the huge pipes of the organ shaking the air, followed by choral voices filling every little space; the life-size statue of Saint Joseph holding a lily; the statue of the Virgin Mary looking up to heaven, her hands joined and her blue scapular falling in folds to the floor.

Over time, the colors and warmth and cleanliness and smoothness and dryness made me aware that not everyone lived with muck and dung and soggy fields or with chilblains and cold and bedsheets that were never fully dry. What had been enkindled inside me was some version of the awe felt by my ancestors when they stepped into a cathedral, and the longing that burned inside them after they returned to their dark, leaky, smoke-filled shelters.

9

PRAYING FOR THE DEAD

Beside my bed, shared with my brother Eddie, Mam knelt with me every night until I knew my prayers by heart.

I was six when "God have mercy on Granny's soul" entered into my bedtime devotions. I loved my grandmother and I knew she loved me.

In the hedge at the far end of Granny's yard an iron gate hung between two glistening granite pillars. Ten feet away, on the other side of the gate, was a single railway track where once a day a fearsome train, big as a mountain, trundled by. One morning, Granny and I stood at the gate waiting, me with clenched hands on a lower bar, while Granny, high above me, held on to the top bar. As the unseen, grunting monster approached between the tall hedges, I could not have borne the mixture of fear and excitement had my grandmother not been with me. I grasped her hand. Then the enormous black engine appeared, blowing out exotic-smelling smoke; the ground shook, and the wagons rattled by on their way to Mountmellick station a mile away. As the train and the noise faded, I saw a stream of water flowing out from under Granny's long black dress.

A few months later Mam slipped silently into our bedroom and knelt beside the bed. "Poor Granny died last night," she said. The gash in my heart has never completely closed. I still see Granny's coffin sinking into the deep and narrow grave, Mam holding my hand.

God have mercy on Paddy Cleary's soul.

Paddy was a young man who oversaw a wheat crusher in Odlum's Mills in Portarlington. On the feast day of the Epiphany, a holy day when the Church demanded abstinence from servile work, Paddy found himself with nothing to do. All his friends were Protestants, and they were working. From a neighbor's farm two fields away he could hear the whine of a mill saw. Paddy had grown up with this neighbor's children, had played cowboys-and-Indians, hide-and-seek, and Sherwood Forest with them, had eaten in their house as often as they had eaten in his. To Paddy, the only difference between Protestants and Catholics was that he got more days off than they did.

The sound of the distant saw on that holy day drew Paddy across the fields. In those years if a man with time on his hands happened on a laboring group of neighbors, he joined in. So Paddy took off his coat and got to work. While he was standing at the end of the table pushing a short piece of tree trunk toward the large whirring saw, the blade broke out of its moorings, and as it flew up into the corrugated roof, it split open Paddy's head. Some Catholics whispered that God punished Paddy Cleary for helping the Protestants on a holy day.

God have mercy on Missus Whittle.

The Owenass River was in flood when old Missus Whittle took the shortcut along the river's bank from Irishtown to the Convent Bridge. In several places the Owenass's earthen pathway twisted around indents made by cattle looking for water in thirsty weather. On the evening when Missus Whittle slipped and fell into one of these drinking holes, the river was eighteen feet wide.

The river in flood was a frightening thing. Its summer depth was a few inches, but after days of rain in the Slieve Bloom Mountains it became a roiling, eddying brown water slithering under the Convent Bridge like a snake that grew bigger every time it sucked up a tributary drain. Sometimes, not even the ten-foot banks were high enough to keep the monster in its place.

It was getting dark when Eddie and I came across a crowd of people milling about on the humpbacked Convent Bridge. Alarm and anxiety were in the air, and we soon heard about Missus Whittle's disappearance. Each of the bridge's parapets was lined with men and women hoping to be the one who spotted her body first. Someone shouted, "There she is, just going under the bridge!" and everyone ran to the opposite side. But it was only a piece of wooden fencing bobbing along.

We squeezed our way into position against the parapet. Even though the sight of the surging river and the idea of seeing the body twisting and turning in the water were terrifying, I clung to the top of the wall and held my place. But unless Missus Whittle was floating, it would be impossible to find her in the dark and speeding water. When I looked straight down, I saw Nurse Byrne kneeling on a coping stone within inches of the rushing flood. She was holding her bicycle lamp a foot above the water, but its weak beam could not pierce the murk.

More than Missus Whittle's drowning, it is the memory of the Jubilee Nurse doing what came naturally that I recall most clearly. In later years, I came to understand that she was searching for a close friend, while knowing that her efforts were in vain and her friend's battered body was being swept like a sodden sack along the bottom of the river.

God have mercy on Peter Collins.

One Sunday Dad took Mam and the five children in the pony-and-trap to a football match in Tullamore in County Offaly. County Laois was playing, and the road from Mountmellick was spotted with horse carts, pony carts, donkey carts, pony traps, and bicycles.

When a lorry passed us, with sides almost as high as a man and flying the blue and white county colors, the jam-packed group of young men on board roared, "Up Laois!" Our pony, Red, flung his startled head into the air, but Dad kept a strong grip on the reins.

A man on a bike was holding on to the side of the lorry, using it to pull him along. "That's Peter Collins holding a tiger's tail," Dad said.

An hour later, when we saw the Tullamore water tower in the distance, Dad said, "There's a whole lot of people on the road up ahead. Something must have happened."

The lorry with the Laois flag had stopped, its tailboard was down, and it was empty. Dad opened the door at the back of the trap and got out to lead the volatile Red through the milling crowd. When they moved aside to let the trap pass by, I saw Peter Collins lying still on the grassy bank. There were deep marks on his ashen face.

God have mercy on Pakie Moore.

In the early 1950s the Industrial Revolution finally reached rural Ireland, and its most ubiquitous symbols were the grey Ford and Massey Ferguson tractors. Some people believed that not only were farm horses gone forever but also that the farmer had been removed from contact with the soil. Now, perched on his tractor, he sailed along on a seat three feet above the fecund, life-giving clay that for millennia had transmitted its placid goodness through his skin and into his soul.

The protective steel cage that now surrounds tractor drivers was devised in the 1960s because so many inexperienced drivers caused their machines to flip over and crush them. Pakie Moore was not in touch with his tractor's center of gravity when he attached it with a steel rope to a tree stump that he intended to pull out of the ground. He backed up to the stump, pushed the accelerator lever as high as possible, and then took his foot off the clutch. When the tractor snapped to a sudden standstill, the front reared off the ground and came back over the rear wheels. The steering wheel cut Pakie in two. His death revived the debate over whether the old ways of farming were safer than the new ones.

God bless Mammy, Daddy, and my sisters and brothers. Amen.

Mam hugged me and ran her fingers through my hair. I climbed into bed knowing that while I slept my guardian angel would have her protective wings spread over me.

❧ 10 ☙

THE STORYTELLER

Up the lane and on the way to the town, a straw-thatched, whitewashed cottage with a gravel front yard snuggled among tall whitethorns. The eaves of the thatch came almost to the tops of the three windows, making the house look like Father McCluskey glaring from under his beetling brows.

Missus Fitz and her husband, Paud, lived there. If Missus Fitz had been a witch she couldn't have baked us in her oven because she didn't have one. Nor did she have a fireplace; her fire was on the hearth under the chimney, which had a square-foot opening at the top. The wall behind the fire was coated in thick soot. Over the years, the rain coming down the chimney had polished the soot, and it glistened and reflected the short flames of the burning turf. Most of the heat given off by the fire was sucked up into the countryside, but somehow Missus Fitz baked her bread and cooked the dinner even if, at times, rain was falling onto her pots and pans, sizzling and hissing like the snakes I'd seen in *Tarzan*.

"Missus Fitz wears her topcoat in the house because she doesn't have much meat on her bones," Dad said.

There was no ceiling in the house, just the underside of the thatched roof. Sometimes a short piece of straw floated down out of the darkness and settled into a teacup. The rafters were ancient, rough-hewn poles, black from decades of turf smoke.

Missus Fitz was very tall. From top to bottom she dressed in black, and the hem of her dress touched her calves. Her ankles were too thin to fill her purplish stockings, and she limped because of a broken hip that had been badly set. "I should have gone to the vet," she joked.

Her grey hair was kept in place with long staples, shaped like the ones Dad used to attach barbed wire to fence posts, only hers were thinner and longer. Her face was as wrinkled as the skin of an old potato lost in the dark for years, and her fingers and the backs of her hands looked like crinkly, brown butter paper.

In the vegetable garden at the back of her house Missus Fitz grew onions. When she harvested them she wove their haulms together into skeins, three onions on top of three onions until the cluster was twelve onions high. Then she hung them on nails in the chimney.

"She always has the smell of onions on her," Dad complained. Dad hated onions.

Poor as a church mouse, Missus Fitz was as proud as a peacock. One time Dad sent me in the pony's cart up to her house with a sack of midwinter potatoes. Dad was being neighborly, but Missus Fitz saw his kindness as charity. She insisted on giving me a half-crown "for delivering the spuds."

When I showed Dad the coin, he snarled, "I told you not to take any money from her." Then he added, "I hope she chokes on them."

One corner of Missus Fitz's front yard was fenced with three-foot-high chicken wire, and in there grew a profusion of fairy-tale colors sending forth fairy-tale smells. A laburnum tree, with its yellow chandeliers, overhung the flower garden and shed its light onto every petal below.

"What's she looking at?" Dad asked Mam when he saw Missus Fitz standing on the lane for a long time.

"Her garden," Mam said. "Her flowers are the only bit of pleasure she has."

Missus Fitz came to her door every morning when she heard us on our way to school. "Learn well," she'd say, or "Study hard," or "Pay attention." Often she'd add, "Remember, yee'll all have to take turns reading to me when I'm old and blind." To me, she'd sometimes say, "When you're a priest, Tom Phelan, you'd better remember me in your first mass or I'll come back to haunt ya." Then she'd turn to my younger brother: "Don't forget you promised to push me wheelchair when me oul spindles give out."

Every day except Sunday, Missus Fitz limped down the hundred yards to our house to get fresh water and milk. First, she filled her white enamel bucket from the farmyard pump and left it outside the wicket door on the lane. Then she came to the kitchen door and called, "Are you home, Nan?" She always waited for Mam to answer, "Come in, Missus Fitz."

Mam liked to hear Missus Fitz's voice because the old woman had the gift of turning her life's pains into laughter. In private, Missus Fitz confided to Mam some of the deep verbal cuts inflicted by her drunken husband, whom she never referred to as anything but Yer Man. But she was never downcast in front of the children.

Every Thursday, Missus Fitz limped into the town to clean Doctor McSharry's office. She wore her good topcoat, the head of a fox on each lapel threatening with its beady eyes. The fox-bodies, attached to the collar to keep Missus Fitz's neck warm, frightened my sisters. But I liked to touch the foxes because they were wild once, had traveled the fields at night, sneaked into henhouses, and run off with dinner for their kits.

On her visits to the town Missus Fitz picked up volumes of gossip, and so her Friday visits to our house were her newsiest. Sitting on the little hob to accommodate her hip, she dispensed the latest dirt to Mam. "Father Kelly and Father Minogue nearly murdered each other outside the priests' house last Monday. Fists flying like two drunk tinkers."

Missus Fitz brought fearless gaiety into our house when Dad was not there. In different accents, she told stories about Kitty the Hare, which she had read in *Ireland's Own,* and stories about banshees and pookas and nasty leprechauns and badly behaved fairies. But she edited and softened the stories for young ears; there was no coarse language except for a "bloody" now and then. We children loved to hear Missus Fitz swear, but if we ever said "bloody," Mam would reach for the rod under the high mantelpiece, or Dad would give us a whack across the side of the head, squishing an ear between hard hand and hard skull.

When Missus Fitz was present and Dad was absent, there was loud, unrestrained laughter in our kitchen. But if Dad was in the farmyard the merriment was subdued. In Dad's struggle to extract a living from the land, there was little room for joy. As well as that, if God saw people being too happy he would send heavy rains and high winds to put them in their place. Whenever Dad barged into the kitchen clanging buckets while Missus Fitz was visiting, she'd say, "Hello JohnJoe." Then she'd get up and go home.

"That one," Dad would say, "keeping everyone from their jobs. Tom, put your boots on and scrape the mangels."

Unlike Dad, Mam had a wonderful sense of humor. She even laughed at his angry encounters with people when enough time had passed and nothing remained but his spluttering and dung-fork waving and the daft things he had shouted.

Missus Fitz had such a miserable life with Yer Man that the only way she endured her lot was to coat it with laughter. She was a true alchemist who could change the vilest misery into fun.

One of us always accompanied Missus Fitz out through the wicket door when she left for home. I often stood there looking at her limping up the lane with her two-flowered milk jug in one hand

and her long body listing against the weight of the water bucket in the other. She could have been the leaning mast of a weather-beaten vessel holding gladly the port, though shrouds and tackle torn, as your man Milton said.

In 1950, Mam, with her turkey profits, replaced the two-wicked wall-lamp in our kitchen with an Aladdin Mantle Lamp. About fifteen times brighter than the two-wicker, the new light was so bright that the children ran outside to look in through the window.

On that winter evening when the lamp made its debut, Missus Fitz was sitting on the little hob. She clapped and exclaimed as the children oohed and aahed at the new crisp shadows on the walls.

Missus Fitz said, "It's like when Cosby Hall put up a windmill to make electric, and they had a light in every room on Christmas Eve. Everyone in Stradbally went by ass-and-cart or horse-and-cart or on shank's mare up to the Windy Gap to admire the lights in Cosby Hall and to imagine they were looking at a ship as big as the *Titanic* on the sea before it sank. For hours we stayed there in the cold."

When Missus Fitz was leaving with her jug of milk on that night of the new lamp, Mam accompanied her onto the lane to her white enamel water bucket, which the children knew Boxer had polluted while waiting for his mistress.

THREE MONTHS LATER, Missus Fitz on the hob told us the further adventures of that night. "Didn't the white light from the new lamp make me as blind as Tim Coughlin on his knees cutting his acre of oats with his sickle, one handful at a time? When Mam left me on the lane with me water and milk, I couldn't see me nose from the brightness in the kitchen; all I was seeing was the white spot after looking at the sun. But I says to meself, I'd been up and down Laragh Lane six thousand times, and I could go home with me eyes shut, so off I went and the next thing everything changed in a flash. I didn't feel any pain at all. I didn't feel meself falling out of the sky.

I didn't know what happened to me jug and bucket. After a few minutes it dawned on me I was lying on my back on something cold. Then I was afraid one of Kitty the Hare's fairies had picked me up and laid me down in the muck like it was laying out me corpse for its wake and I was not even dead yet. It was the smell that told me I was in the drain. Once a year your father cleans up that drain and everyone in Laragh knows he's doing it because the stink spreads all over the place; the drain is full of the clay and rotting snags from the potatoes that flow across under the lane when yer father washes them in the trough at the pump for the pigs. But to this very day I can't say how I got into the drain; it had to be a fairy. I said to meself, I better get out of here before the fairies think I'm dead and start winding the rosary beads through me fingers and tying me jaw shut with a rag and putting pennies on me eyelids. I struggled like an oul hen when you hold it by the head, but I couldn't get a move out of meself. There I was, looking up at the dark. Then I felt the cold, wet muck seeping in through me clothes and through me hair, too, onto me poor oul skull. I thought, This is worse than lying on the floor of a pighouse where the pigs do their business."

ABOUT HALF AN hour after Missus Fitz left for home on the night of the brilliant light, Dad came into the kitchen with the yard lamp hanging out of his hand. We children were all at the table doing our homework. With a wink and a nod of the head, he told Mam he needed to talk to her outside. We all cocked our ears, but Mam closed the kitchen door as she left. My little brother ran to the door, put his ear to it, and ran back grinning to his place at the table.

"Dad said Tom's a pig like this," he said, and he pushed up his nose, exposed the inside of his nostrils. We all sniggered and oinked except my sister, who *tsked* in disgust.

In the farmyard Dad asked Mam to listen for a minute because he thought he'd heard someone talking outside the high corrugated gate. Dad was afraid of the dark, afraid of creatures that might be in the dark, and afraid of whispered voices in the dark.

MISSUS FITZ ON the hob continued her saga. "If nothing else, it was the smell that made me want to get out of the ditch. But before I even made a stir I started fretting at what Yer Man would say when I hobbled into the kitchen at home, above smelling like the back end of a calf with the scour. But when I tried to stand up I knew me leg was broke. As well as that, I was so stuck in the muck that I couldn't even sit up, the suction was so bad, like when your wellington gets stuck in the bog. As Kitty the Hare would say, I was as stuck as a tick in a tinker's bum. I called for Mam, but I was three feet down in the ditch, and then there was the width of the lane, and then the wicket door, and then the kitchen door stopping me shouts. Boxer just stood there on the bank looking down, he wouldn't even bark. I kept saying 'Will you bark, you eejit? Bark, you useless bag of bones!' I got so hoarse calling Mam that I nearly gave up, and I began to think I was going to die at the bottom of the ditch, covered with the terrible black muck, and no one would know what happened to me until your father cleaned out the drain the next year and found me preserved like the body of a saint. Saint Moll Fitzpatrick, and me with my picture on a holy card with me eyes turned up to heaven and me hands joined and a golden halo around me head. I would be the patron saint of people who fall in mucky ditches if there isn't one already." Missus Fitz swiped her nose with the rag she always carried in her right hand.

MAM TOOK THE yard lamp and led Dad to the high gate. They listened. They heard a voice saying, "Bark, you fucking useless bag of fucking bones!" Then she shouted, "Nan! I'm in the ditch!"

"It's Missus Fitz!" Mam rushed out onto the lane with Dad following. "Where are you, Missus Fitz?"

*   *   *

MISSUS FITZ SNIFFED at the rag in her fist and continued her side of the story. "When I heard Mam calling me, I said, 'Oh, Jesus be praised! I'm over here, Nan.'

"When Mam saw where I was, she handed the lamp to your father and lowered herself into the ditch, stepped across me, turned around, bent down, pushed her arms in under me oul bones, and lifted me up. The sound of the sucking of the muck! I was afraid your father would think I was blurting. Then she put me lying on me back on the grass verge. To your father's credit he never said a word, didn't ask me what I was doing in the ditch like Yer Man did later on."

WITH MISSUS FITZ safely on the grass, Dad hurried into the kitchen and told us Missus Fitz had fallen into the ditch and hurt her leg. "She has brittle bones," he said.

He lit the old two-wicker lamp and said, "Gather up your books and come with me." He led us into the parlor, then warned us, "Don't be coming back into the kitchen until I tell you to."

ATOP THE HOB, Missus Fitz went on with her version of the adventure. "By the time your father let youse out of the parlor, Mam was up at our house telling Yer Man what happened. Tom said, 'The stink of you, Missus Fitz!' And there I was sitting in the very chair Mam bought at the dead priest's auction feeling like a pig that just came out of his mud puddle and feeling terrible sorry for meself. I looked like a witch with me long hair down me back because Mam had to open me bun to get out the dirt; me oul stockings were down around me ankles with the weight of the muck and me oul skinny legs no ticker than a briar on display. And Tom was right; I was pure stink. All the back of me was coated in black muck even though Mam had scraped most of it off with the edge of the bread knife. And ye all stood around me gaping and silent, and for something to say I says, 'I broke me leg.' And one of ye said, 'What leg?' and someone else said, 'Did it crack out loud like a rotten stick?' and another said, 'Can we look at the bone sticking out?'

"Mam arrived back in the kitchen and said, 'Paud's on his way, Missus Fitz.'

"'Did he say anything, Nan?' I asked.

"'He did,' Mam replied, but she did not tell me what it was."

DAD BANGED IN through the kitchen door with two poles and leaned them against the wall near the clock. "About five minutes, Nan," he said and left. I wondered what five minutes he was talking about.

Mam got her old yard coat and gave it to me to hold. Then she began to pull Missus Fitz's arms out of the sleeves of her stinky coat. Missus Fitz used the arms of the chair to lift herself off the seat and Mam slipped the coat from under her. "Oh, Nan," she said, "don't let the lads see me oul knickers."

Dad came back and said, "Everything's ready. How's the leg, Missus?"

"All right, JohnJoe," Missus Fitz said, and she made a face that she thought only Dad saw.

Dad used the fireplace tongs to carry Missus Fitz's coat out of the house. No sooner had he come back in and closed the door than an aggressive knock sounded.

"Brace yeerselves, lads," Missus Fitz said. "Here comes Josef Stalin."

Paud Fitzpatrick stepped in without removing his hat, and stood at the corner of the fireplace wall. He was dressed in the same brown wedding suit he had bought thirty-seven years earlier, which now served as his work clothes, waistcoat included. His shirt was collarless. Because his eyes were always slitted like a hunting cat's, because his face muscles were always tense, because he was in perpetual need of a shave, I infused Paud with the personality of a viciously thorned bush. At five feet eight inches, he stood ramrod straight, which made him a freak in a countryside filled with stoop-shouldered farmers. Paud claimed to have been a member of a flying column of the IRA at the time of the British ouster, but Dad said all he ever did was steal porter from a Protestant shop and claim he had made a strike for Irish freedom.

• Paud looked at his wife like she was something the cat had dragged in. "What happened ja?" he demanded, his tone suggesting his wife had jumped into the ditch just to inconvenience him.

"What *happened* me?" Missus Fitz shouted back. "Nan told you what happened me."

"Ya fell in the ditch."

"I fell in the ditch."

"Didja break the milk jug?"

"Feck the jug, yowl shite! I broke me feckin' leg!"

Dad intervened to save the children's ears. "Paud, we'll bring Missus Fitz home in the horse-and-cart. Why don't you go on ahead and get a good fire going so she can dry out a bit and not catch cold?"

Paud threw a glance at Dad, then scraped the soles of his hobnailed boots on the floor like a challenged bull pawing the ground. "Maybe she'll fall into the canal next time and get it over with," he said as he walked out.

✓ ON THE HOB, Missus Fitz snuffed and then continued her story. "I'll live longer than Yer Man yet if it kills me. I was just glad that he didn't say anything that you childers shouldn't be hearing. And the minute he was gone, your father tied the two poles under the dead priest's chair and made a litter like one of them things for carrying around queens, only theirs has sides and roofs and curtains and lads dressed up like clowns hoisting them over puddles and horse dung so they don't get their dainty shoes dirty. And me in me litter and Mam behind and your father in front, I sailed up in the air and they took me out into the yard, and it was like I was on a magic carpet. Your father had the tailboard out and they lifted the litter and me into the cart like I was as light as a feather. And there I was, Queen Victoria herself on top of an elephant in India ready to set out on her grand tour only it was dark and the only light was the yard lamp.

. "Your father lifted two of ye up beside me to make sure I wouldn't fall out of the chair. Wasn't it all grand and me up there in the middle like I was Victoria herself and me leg killing me; Eddie out there in front in the middle of the lane with the lamp like Jesus looking for a lost sheep; your father leading Lame Mare by the winkers like Joseph leading d'ass into Egypt and missing the biggest potholes; Mam walking along with her hand on the sideboard just in case; the two lads beside me like page boys in Buckingham Palace and the girls behind carrying the queen's drinks in case she got thirsty on the long journey to me house a hundred yards up the lane."

YER MAN DIED a decade before Missus Fitz did. She was triumphantly happy "when he went toes up," as she said. As Paud's coffin was lowered into the darkness, she was heard to mutter, "Youl bollicks! If you think I'm going to be planted anywhere near you, then you're still a ferocious feckin' eejit."

Missus Fitz was true to her word. When she died, she was buried in a small cemetery on the far side of the Windy Gap, twenty-three miles from Yer Man.

THE ROAD TO SCHOOL

When my siblings and I stepped out through the farmyard's wicket door, there was Slieve Bloom, our blue mountain, five miles off to the west. Sometimes Slieve Bloom floated on a cloud of low, white mist. In wintertime snow covered her head while the rest of the world stayed green. In summertime, showers lit by the sun swept across her face like a lace mantilla. Some days she would hide behind a curtain of fog and rain. At evening time, when an enormous cloud the same deep blue color as herself rose up behind her, it seemed she was as high as Mount Everest.

Slieve Bloom was always there, a lying-down woman ascending out of the Central Plain, slowly lifting herself up to seventeen hundred feet and then sloping back down to the plain. She was our pole-star. There was nothing beyond her but a breathtaking chasm. After spending the day picking clean the fields of the earth, an unending flight of crows meandered over our house toward the mountain to rookeries known only to them. Every evening a low-flying Aer Lingus plane, a green light on each wing tip, droned by on its jaunt from Dublin to Rineanna before skimming the top of Slieve Bloom and disappearing. On clear evenings the top rim of the setting sun clung to the top rim of the mountain until finally slipping away and leaving us in a long twilight.

Grown-ups could foretell the weather by glancing at Slieve Bloom. But even as a child, I knew that certain clouds rising up over her head would come tumbling down her face, dropping veils of rain that would soon be falling into our farmyard. When the sky was clear and the mountain shimmered, it was a promise of sunny days to come. Whenever Dad announced on a winter morning, "There's snow on the mountain," we ran out to the lane to gape at the wonder that seemed five miles high and a hundred miles distant.

Each morning of my early school days, when I left the cocoon of the farmyard and the protection of Slieve Bloom, I stepped into an alien world beset with traps and snares that I was too naive to recognize until I tripped them.

Our house was at the halfway point on mile-long Laragh Lane, which came to an end beside a dunghill of mountainous grandeur at Durt Donovan's front door. With its muddy tongue, the other end of our road licked the edge of the macadamed Harbour Street. Wide enough for a horse's cart, the lane was a graveled track. The iron-shod wheels of carts and machinery gouged out deep potholes, and since the town end of the lane was used the most, it was there that the potholes were biggest. Throughout my childhood I longed for the county council to make our lane like the streets in the town. Then I could ride my bike without neck-snapping plunges into deep depressions; I would have a smooth surface for my whipping top; in summer I could run barefoot on the road beside the rim of a bicycle wheel and tap it along with a short stick; I could play "followers" without fear of losing the marbles in nettles and briars or having to feel for them in muddy, water-filled ruts.

When it wasn't raining, my siblings and I walked to school. If the lane was dry and dusty we watched out for fresh cattle plops. But after spills of rain it was the potholes of watery cow dung we were wary of.

In the spring, the tiny buds on the hedges were as vivid as the green lights on an aeroplane's wings in the dark; thrushes sang, crows sniffed the countryside from on high, wandering along like dogs trotting from one scent to another. Cock blackbirds screeched and fought each other in the sky, and magpies hopped along the lane in front of us.

A drain ran beside the lane, and in summertime wildflowers and weeds covered its banks in colorful disarray. In the spring its waters supported floats of frog spawn.

"Frog spawn looks like tapioca."

"Don't say that."

"Frog spawn *is* tapioca."

"I'm telling."

Past the tarred, wooden gate in the Meadow Field we meandered between the high bank on the left and the trimmed whitethorn hedge of the Back of Fitzes field on the right. At the beginning of autumn the wild strawberries growing among the grasses in the drain's bank were picked by the finder, brought home in a handkerchief, mashed on a saucer, covered with that morning's cream, sprinkled with sugar, and eaten in solitary greed while the others stood around drooling.

During the leafy spring we kept watch on the nest-building birds in the bushes. Later we hoisted each other onto shoulders to look at the ugly, purple, hairy hatchlings, opening wide their beaks to what they thought was a parent coming with worms. Only a mother could love those scalds, but magpies and grey crows loved them, too, as hors d'oeuvres.

In winter the hedges glittered with hips and haws. It was on this stretch of the lane one winter morning we met Fergus Horgan, a tall, strong man leaving his footprints in the inch of snow. He was crying.

"My father died last night," he said. "I'm going down to tell your mam and dad." I looked after Fergus with my fingertips at my mouth. It was his tears rather than the death of his father that disturbed me; I had not seen grown-up tears in my Arcadia before.

A hundred yards from the Meadow Field gate, we came to Missus Fitz's thatched cottage. The colors and bouquets of her garden were a weak anodyne against her porcine husband, Paud. Once, as my brother and I were passing the house, Paud was standing in the front door lighting his pipe. He flicked the spent, still-smoking match at us.

"Stick that up in the hair of your arse," he said.

Fifty yards beyond the Fitzpatricks', the Furry Hill made a small dip in the road as it descended a shallow deposit of sand left by the last ice age. The furze-covered field on the left belonging to Isaac Thompson gave the hill its name. Most times we ran down the hill, where one dark Sunday morning on my way to serve mass I skidded on black ice and fell backward off my bike and onto my head. I spent several days in bed before I regained my equilibrium.

It was at the foot of the Furry Hill that Dad and I once caught up with his old friend Mister Bannon, home from England for the first time since the end of the First World War. Mister Bannon had fought in the trenches. In a rare display of emotion Dad almost jumped out of the horse's cart when he saw the old soldier. They shook hands and spoke over each other in their excitement. Mister Bannon came home with us, and Mam invited him to stay for supper.

As we ate, one of the children said, "Tell us about the war?"

"Sure I will," Mister Bannon said. "Once in Belgium me and a few lads caught an old hen and killed it. But we had no way to cook it until one of them wild lads from the Wicklow Mountains said he knew what to do. He cut off the legs and the head and plastered the whole thing, feathers and all, with muck. The rest of us gathered sticks and got a great fire going. Your man put the mucky ham into the middle of the blazes. After an hour he broke off the baked mud and there was the hen in its birthday suit. All its feathers had come off with the mud. Then he made a slit in its bum and the guts fell out in a ball. There was great aten, lads. I can still taste it."

Not far from the Furry Hill, Rourke's Bridge spanned Rourke's deep drain. Drunken Uncle Paulie had caught pneumonia in that drain after riding his bike into it on a dark night. On our way home from school, when the water was shallow, we climbed down the bank, stood under the small bridge, and made echoes by whooping like Indians in the pictures.

Next we passed between two fields owned by Lar Dixon. In the drain on the far side of the fence of Murt's field a grazing donkey had once become stuck in the deep muck, worked itself to death trying to get free, and for weeks polluted Laragh with its stink. Nobody could cover the dead animal with soil because the owner refused to allow anyone on his property.

"Don't put one foot on my land. Don't touch *my* drain or I'll have the law on you!"

"It's not your drain, you gobshite," Dad said.

"Don't put one of your feet on my property or I'll have you arrested!"

Eventually, Dad and Podge Nolan rubbed some Vicks under their noses on the night of a half-moon and buried the donkey where it had died.

On the other side of the lane, in the Well Field, Lar Dixon's horse had galloped in the dark into a handle of his misplaced plough and mortally wounded itself. We trailed our big sister around the corner and up onto the Canal Line. In single file we walked on the side of the lane farthest from the Canal Bank. We knew a boogie man lived in the weedy water waiting to grab children by the shoelaces and pull them in.

This branch of the Grand Canal was four and a half feet deep in the middle and thirty feet wide, except at the Harbour, where it was deeper and sixty feet wide to allow for barges to dock and turn. The Canal came to an end at the top of Laragh Lane. The Canal Company could fine people for damaging the banks, washing dogs, washing clothes, washing one's person or the person of another, and for stealing water from the Canal.

Across the Harbour, a large, four-storied warehouse sat at the edge of the water like a rough-hewn Venetian palazzo. Above the high black doors in the center of the store's facade, a large awning of corrugated iron allowed for the unloading of merchandise from the barges in wet weather.

We passed under the overhanging elderberry bush that Dad and the diminutive Canal inspector quarreled about. Dad told the inspector that the low-hanging branches knocked his hat off every time he trotted by in the pony-and-cart, and he asked him to cut them back. The inspector may have been minute in size, but in aggression he was a yellow-beaked cock blackbird defending his territory.

"That elderberry bush belongs to the Canal Company."

"But it's growing out over the lane. Couldn't you cut it back?"

"No."

"Then I'll come up with my billhook and chop the whole thing down and throw it in the canal."

"If you touch that bush I'll have—"

"—the law with the full weight of the Canal Company's lawyers after you," Dad joined in.

Dad did not cut down the bush, but every time he went by he broke off a branch until he had established safe passage for his hat.

When the summers were dry, Dad "borrowed" water from the Canal for his cattle, first hauling it away in fifty-gallon drums and then eventually inserting a pipe through the Canal Bank to siphon off water. The children were used as lookouts for the little runt during the operation.

Where the Canal ended, a quay made of large coping stones allowed for the transferring of sacks of barley and turf from horses' carts onto the barges. The lane turned sharply and ran between the edge of this quay and the Harbour Master's two-story house with its overhanging eaves. Whenever the Harbour Master saw us approaching, he stepped away from supervising the loading of the barges to guide us safely through the horses and carts with their sacks of barley and creels of turf. On quiet mornings, his wife sometimes raised a window to say hello. But whenever she did, her unexpected and elevated voice never failed to give my sister a start.

"Holy mother of God!" she would cry, clasping her chest like she was at the Consecration of the mass.

Just beyond the house, Laragh Lane ran out onto Harbour Street. After a hundred yards of smooth macadamed surface we passed Mister Lowndes's public house, grocery, and farm supply shop on the right. It was here Dad and Mam bought the weekly messages and animal feed. Mister Lowndes killed and butchered our pig every year and helped with the saving of our hay. In return, Dad loaned him horses and bogies when it was time for him to bring the hay home from his small farm. But there had been a disastrous falling-out.

As it did with many consumer items, the Irish government controlled the price of paraffin oil. On a certain Monday in the 1950s the cost of a gallon was set to increase by a halfpenny. On the Saturday before, I had been sent to Lowndes's for paraffin. I was charged the new price. When Dad heard about it he spewed lava at Mister Lowndes. All commercial, social, and neighborly contact came to a sudden stop. Even Mam's friendly relationship with Missus Lowndes was no longer sustainable.

What was it about this harmless error that caused Dad to react so angrily? I did not understand how one halfpenny could cause such a war. Later I would come to see that many people in rural Ireland did not have the skills to negotiate. Instead, confrontations were followed by avoidance, and the hard feelings went unresolved even as both parties settled into eternity, close together six feet below the surface of the local cemetery.

What caused my deep apprehension when passing Lowndes's shop was not the halfpenny war; it was the spookiness I attached to the area after Peter Doheny smashed one of the plateglass windows in Lowndes's shop with a heavy piece of wood. According to the schoolyard grapevine, Mister Doheny roared as he was subdued, tied up in a straitjacket, and brought to Saint Dympna's Asylum in Carlow.

In my mind, I was unable to separate the anguished screams of Mister Doheny from the roars coming out of our middle house when Uncle Jack was subduing a fully grown bull. As if I had been at the scene, I heard Mister Doheny shouting while big men held him down on the hard road and rendered him as powerless as a Christmas turkey with its wings and feet strapped to its body. That area of Harbour Street forever retained the terror I imbued it with when I was a child peering at the harshness of life through the cracks in the protective walls the adults had built around me.

Across the street from Lowndes's was a long, low thatched house with small curtained windows keeping watch on all who passed by. Often on our way home from school, Missus Rourke was standing in the doorway, waiting to invite us in out of the rain or for a biscuit or to see newborn kittens or pups. Later I would wonder if she was trying to defuse the animosity that existed between her husband and Dad because of a drain, animosity that would flare into open war in times to come.

Harbour Street ran into Lord Edward Street, with Joey Hayden's shop the boundary line. In one of Joey's large windows a dusty pyramid of sun-faded Persil boxes maintained its balance for all the years of my elementary schooling. Across the street from the shop, Missus Cooney was often seen resting on her half-door. Her house was like a picture in the Peter Rabbit book Aunt Teresa had sent for my third birthday. The roof was thatch, the chimney smoke was blue, the walls were white, the quoins and window frames black. A pot of red geraniums sat on each of the two windowsills. "I knew your Mam and Dad when they were children," Missus Cooney once told us.

Just beyond Missus Cooney's was the row of attached, two-storied, redbrick houses called the Artisans' Dwellings. Mister Duffy, shell-shocked in the First World War, lived in one of them. When his terrors overcame him, his shrieks and shouts were frightening, so we never walked on his side of the street. Farther along, another veteran, Mister Collins, struggled with crutches and an ill-fitting wooden leg. Sometimes we met Mick Kerwin, the postman, limping his way from door to door; he, too, had lost a leg in the war.

I envied the children who lived in the Artisans' Dwellings. They had a tarred street to whip their tops and ride their bikes on; they didn't have to keep looking down to avoid muck or dung as they walked. It would be a long time before I realized that not all the parents in those houses could afford whipping tops, let alone bicycles.

Near the far end of Lord Edward Street, the ancient John Nannery and his hunchbacked sister, Joan, ran a small sweet shop. When the schools closed, children crowded in to spend their pennies on Peggy's Leg, Fizz Bags, Black Jack, Lucky Bags, and Bull's Eyes. When someone muttered "Humpy" within the safety of a group, the shop was immediately cleared of the innocent and the guilty, and the children were told to come back in two at a time to buy their sweets.

Lord Edward Street split into a Y at Mansfield's Pub. When I was in third class, I found a red sponge ball behind the ball alley at the National School. Fat Arthur Mansfield, who lived above the pub, tried to pull it out of my hands. When I wouldn't give it up, he said, "If you don't bring it to school tomorrow, I'll paralyze you!"

I never told anyone at home about Fat Arthur, because I would have been commanded to give him the ball so he wouldn't beat me up. After his threat, whenever I was sent to town for the messages, I gathered up speed on my bike as I neared Mansfield's Pub just in case Fat Arthur was lurking.

Lord Edward's right leg bent and went over the Owenass by way of the Convent Bridge and on toward the town. One night while standing at the parapet, drunken Uncle Paulie got tired carrying his box of weekly groceries and heaved it into the river below.

The Presentation Convent School abutted the riverbank. There I spent my first four years of school under the kind and patient tutelage of those dedicated nuns.

Lord Edward's left leg became Connolly Street, and where that quickly became Acragar Road, the Boys' National School sat behind a four-foot wall. Here were my Etonian playing fields, and here I also became acquainted with the casual violence and boisterous brutality of the schoolyard. Here Slieve Bloom could not be seen and I was left to find my own way in a strange world.

FIRST BABIES

All the Catholic children in Mountmellick began their formal education in the Presentation Convent School on the west bank of the Owenass River. The Protestant children, whom we Catholics never saw, had their own building farther up the town. It was the 1940s, and the Church was so afraid of defections that she forbade her members, under pain of mortal sin, from attending Protestant schools as well as weddings and funerals.

When I was four, I was placed in the "First Babies" classroom. After living on the outer edge of the town in semiseclusion with my siblings, I was intrigued by all the new faces. My teacher, Sister Genevieve, looked cross in her glinting glasses, but she was a kind woman who quietly convinced the frightened or crying or loose-sphinctered or unruly or already streetwise boys and girls that they were safe with her, that she would take care of them until their parents or older siblings came to take them home. She smelled like the flowers in Missus Fitz's garden.

At lunchtime on my first day, I stood in the enclosed concrete schoolyard with my back to the pebble-dashed walls, watching a screaming whirlpool of children spinning around in the small playground, delighted at being released from the prison of classroom obedience. Soon I tentatively stepped into the outer circle and was quickly sucked into the rapturous eddy.

The appearance of an old, plump nun brought everyone to a sudden stop. With grandmotherly kindness spilling out of her deep wrinkles, Sister Conception held a dinner plate covered with tiny squares of buttered and jammed bread. Like chickens fluttering to a scattered handful of crushed oats, the children mobbed her and begged to be chosen. On that first day I got one of the tasty morsels, and when Sister Conception bent down to me, she said, "You're Sister de Sales's nephew, aren't you? You'll be a grand priest."

My religious indoctrination began in Sister Genevieve's class. I listened attentively and believed innocently. I was taught how to perform my first religious rite—making the sign of the cross.

"Children, you can only bless yourself with your right hand. It's a sign of the devil to bless yourself with your left. Now, everyone, raise your right hand!" Half the class raised their left.

I learned that God is everywhere and that the sun shines and the rain falls because God causes everything to happen. I chanted the Hail Mary and the Glory Be. I learned to bow my head every time I said or heard the word "Jesus," and I learned that my guardian angel walked beside me, protecting me from the devil. Sister showed us a picture of an angel with its wings spread over a sleeping child in a bedroom that looked far nicer than mine, one where there were no overcoats spread on the bed to keep the child warm. I learned I had to pray to my guardian angel every day: *Angel of God, my guardian dear, to whom God's love commits me here, ever this day, be at my side to light and guard, to rule and guide. Amen.*

Our teacher also taught us songs and stories about crows and foxes and saints and hares and tortoises, ants and crickets, lions and mice. Sometimes the lions and mice and guardian angel and crows and foxes and saints became entangled in my head, and the lion became the mouse-saving guardian angel.

The class counted to ten while Sister Genevieve's pointer hopped from number to number on the blackboard, and I found comfort in the recitation, in the sing-songedness of the voices. In the herd I was as good as everyone else.

In the First Babies classroom there were no smells of dampness or farmyard or dunghill. Instead, a snug atmosphere was created by the wood-paneled walls coated in linseed oil; wooden floorboards impregnated with decades of dust; sunbeams slanting down from window to floor; the nun's eau de cologne; the new books and the children's new school clothes.

But in this Eden there was a dragon. On that first day in school as I whirled in the playground with all the other screaming children, I fell and skinned my knees. Paddy Connors, a boy from the town, saw me struggling with tears. "You're only an oul girl," he shouted for all to hear. As I made my way to the wall he continued jeering, which soon attracted a chorus of blood-pecking fowl. "Oul girl! Oul girl! Oul girl!"

As much as I liked my classes, I did not enjoy the social aspect of school. Most of the pupils had been reared in the town, had to some extent grown up on the streets. While I was wearing my wellingtons, dressed in a hand-me-down smock, and doing my jobs in the farm-yard, they had learned to play with each other—and fight with each other. And they knew who *not* to fight.

In glaring comparison, I was socially retarded. I did not know the rules of engagement, did not know being called a dirty oul farmer could be ignored. At first, I ran to adults for protection from chil-dren I found threatening, and this behavior, along with my being a farmer's son, gave me the plumage of a different-colored bird, one who attracted the pecking beaks and sharp claws of the birds of a constant feather.

Paddy Connors evolved into the most aggressive bully during my years in elementary school. But I never told Mam and Dad about him, not even when he gave me the Indian torture, or knelt on my chest and flattened my nose with the palm of his hand, or put his hand up the leg of my short trousers and twisted my mickey.

On that first day of school, when Mam asked how I got on, I breathlessly told her, "Seanie McCoy fainted and fell out of his seat and onto the floor and got all white and the nun waved a book in front of his face to make the wind cold!"

13

THE PENNY CATECHISM

As a child I loved the feeling of conquest when I committed multiplication tables, poems, songs, and riddles to memory. But trying to memorize the answers to the Penny Catechism questions was as painful as forcing a path through a stand of blackthorn bushes on a dark winter's night. Its words were assembled in lawyerly language unsuited to a young mind. There was no music, no rhythm, no comfort. Chanting the text in class quickly became a cacophony as thirty children wrestled with tongue-tying words that were coal cinders in the mouth: ex cathedra, eucharistic, plenary, absolution, contrition, conception, canonization, resurrection, Transfiguration, Annunciation, Assumption, transubstantiation, consubstantiation, venial, mystical, infallibility, brimstone, purgatory, adultery, penitential, matrimonial, temporal, conditional, Beelzebub, calumny, Pentecost, indulgences, Epistle, Epiphany, Extreme Unction, seraphim, cherubim, dominions, principalities.

The lowly title "Penny Catechism" did not come from the bishops of Ireland who oversaw its composition. They called their effort the *Catechism of Catholic Doctrine Approved by the Archbishops and Bishops in Low Week, 1911, for Infants and Standard 1.*

The Penny Catechism was our introduction to the Church's dogma and its interpretation of the Ten Commandments. As this theology was absorbed, I developed a sense of guilt about breaking the sacred rules. Disobeying my parents, lying to my teacher to avoid being whacked with a hazel stick, and wishing Paddy Connors would drop dead put dark stains on my soul.

Mam and Dad believed there was nothing worse than failing at catechism.

"Aren't you ashamed of yourself, and your aunt Teresa a nun? Not knowing your catechism, and throwing stones at a cat in the town where everyone could see you!"

The nuns in our local convent belonged to the same order as Aunt Teresa, and Dad and Mam imagined that gossipy letters about the Phelan offspring flew daily from Mountmellick to my aunt's convent.

Many mornings when Mam was not convinced I knew my catechism homework, she rousted me out of bed and sent me to the cow house, where Dad was milking one of our five cows. Three semiferal cats waiting for their morning treat reluctantly moved as I made my way to the extra milking stool.

"Who made you?"

"God made me."

"Why did God make you?"

"To love, honor, and obey Him here on earth and live happily with Him forever in heaven."

"Say that one again."

I stumbled through the responses until I finally got them right. Sometimes when Dad lost patience with me, he squirted me in the face with milk straight out of the cow's pap. I may have gone to school knowing why God made me, but the stink of sour milk wafting off me reminded the town children, as if they needed reminding, to call me a smelly oul farmer.

WHEN I GRADUATED to the Boys School, I discovered that once a year the diocesan examiner, Father Kaye, visited each classroom to ensure we were being successfully indoctrinated. This was a day of high anxiety. Under threat of visitation from the hazel rod, everyone was on good behavior. Everyone was dressed in their Sunday best which, for some, meant wearing their long-outgrown First Communion suit. There were many ripped seams and choking collars.

When Father Kaye entered the classroom, we became as still as a school of perch in the canal. Then we all stood.

"Good morning, children."

"Good mornin', Faaa-der."

"Please, sit down, boys."

Father Kaye's freshly shaved face was aglow and his hair was like painted waves in the picture of Jesus on the Sea of Galilee. His hands were so clean that I knew no soil or weed sap had ever stained his fingers. His Roman collar gleamed, his spotless suit was a perfect fit, the trousers creased. His shoes were shining brightly.

Father Kaye had never worn a patched coat over his head when it rained nor walked through muck and cow dung and hen dung and duck dung and turkey dung in leaking wellingtons. He had never scraped the clay off mangels with a broken kitchen knife while kneeling on a cold floor in a cold shed. He had never prepared buckets of mash for winter cattle nor flung animal dung through a barn window.

Father Kaye turned every catechism answer to the credit of the child no matter how senseless it was.

"Next boy . . . How many sacraments are there?"

"A-leven, Faaa-der."

"Seven . . . very good."

"Next boy . . . What's an angel?"

"A big white burd with a ring around its head."

"Very good. Angels remind me of birds, too."

When the ordeal was over, Father Kaye congratulated the teacher and the students. Then he said, "You are a very polite group of boys. Your parents work hard to dress you in such grand clothes, so be sure to love and obey them."

We knew Father Kaye liked us. He was not like our parish priest, Father McCluskey, who snapped and snorted and snarled and growled at everyone in a mixture of Irish and English. I knew that when I became a priest, I would be kind like Father Kaye. I would be clean and gentle and never raise my voice to children.

14

SCARY SURPRISE FROM
THE DARK CONTINENT

One day when I was in First Class, Sister Martha opened the door of the tall cabinet with a dramatic flourish to reveal a statue of Blessed Martin de Porres of Peru. She said that if we brought a penny for the Black Babies in Africa and dropped it into the slot at Blessed Martin's feet, he would nod his head in thanks. Then she told us how Martin could talk to dogs and cats and mice, float in the air, walk through locked doors, and be in two places at the same time.

"Sister! My father talks to our ass and tells it to 'hupp and go,' and the ass does it," Jack Deegan said.

"Sister! If I could float in the air, I'd get the high apples off the apple tree in Father McCluskey's garden," Billy Marshall said.

"Sister! If I could be in two places at the same time, one of me would stay in bed all day warm, an' I'd send the other one to school," Sheila Feeney said.

Besides pennies for Black Babies, Sister Martha encouraged us to bring in cancelled stamps and silver paper from the insides of cigarette boxes for the foreign missions. Thus the Irish mania for the

conversion of happy pagans into miserable Catholics was instilled in
me at an early age.

When Sister Martha taught us to sing a hymn, she began by
whacking her tuning fork on the edge of her desk and then humming till her hum matched that of the fork. Still humming, she put
down the tuning fork, walked to the center of the classroom, hummed
louder, and used her hands to tell us children to hum along with her.
As we took up the hum, she pointed to the blackboard where she had
written the verses of the hymn. With her bobbing head, she counted
out, "One, two, three!" And then waved us into song.

"Hail, Queen of heav'n, the ocean star!

"Guide of the wand'rer here below!—"

Suddenly a demanding knock on the classroom door interrupted
our uplifted voices. When Sister Martha opened it, a priest was
standing in the corridor holding a suitcase. As he stepped into the
room, we stood up and bleated, "Good morning, Fa-aa-ther."

"Good morning, children. You may sit down," the priest said,
smiling at the room of seven- and eight-year-olds. I could see he was
not thorny like Father McCluskey.

"Children!" Sister Martha said. "This is Father Dalton and he is
home from the foreign missions. He's going to tell us about his life
in a country in Africa that's full of jungles and monkeys and zebras
and elephants."

Having a real live missionary in our classroom was almost as
exciting as a visit from a clown in Duffy's Circus.

Father Dalton plonked his suitcase on Sister Martha's desk. Then
he opened it slowly, as if something might jump out and bite him. I
held my breath.

"You are the first children to see my surprise from Africa," he
said. Carefully, he put his hands in the suitcase and began to draw
out a piece of cloth the color of burnt orange, with diamond shapes
made by two black lines crisscrossing each other. He moved away
from the suitcase and the cloth kept coming. Slowly he walked

backward through the rows of desks until he was at the rear wall, one end of the cloth in his hands and the other end still in the suitcase.

I was goggle-eyed at this un-priestly behavior.

"Who can tell me what this is?" Father Dalton asked.

Wagging hands filled the air.

"A scarf for a giant?"

"No."

"Wallpaper?"

"No . . . I'll give you a hint: *hisssssssss.*"

"A goose?" a chorus of children sang out.

"No."

"A cross cat," a boy yelled.

"No."

"A bike wheel after someone rides over a bush that's full of thorns?"

"No," Father Dalton said. "It's a snakeskin."

He may as well have said "It's a lion that hasn't eaten a child for a month."

Screeching and screaming, all the girls and boys scrambled out of their chairs and pressed themselves in bunches against the classroom walls.

Sister Martha laid down a blanket of calmness by walking over to the snakeskin and running the flat of her hand along it. "See," she said, "it's not alive." But at that moment, as if to show how wrong she was, Father Dalton sent a ripple running along the hide of the dead reptile.

As the children teetered on the edge of hysteria, Sister Martha gave the priest a withering look, as if to ask, "What kind of a fecking eejit are you?"

Then she lifted the end of the snakeskin out of the suitcase and began to roll it up. The priest had no choice but to do the same from his end.

When the suitcase was firmly hasped, Father Dalton asked if any of the children were going to be missionaries when they got big.

"Would there be snakes, Fadder?"

The priest looked at Sister Martha. "Are there any snakes in Ireland, children?" she asked.

"Nooooo, Sister."

"Who drove the snakes out of Ireland, children?"

"Saint Pa-aa-trick," chorused thirty-four mouths.

"And why did he drive them out?"

Only one girl answered. "Because they frighten little children, Sister."

Sister Martha looked at the priest. "Isn't that right, Father? Snakes frighten little children?"

"That's right, Sister. But it was just a ski—"

Sister Martha interrupted him. "Out of the mouths of babes, Father," she said, and she raised her eyebrows into spears.

Father Dalton lifted his suitcase off Sister Martha's desk, and the nun waved us children to our feet as he left.

"Goodbye, Fa-aa-ther."

We all sat down.

"We'll start the hymn again, children," Sister Martha said. She held up her tuning fork for all to see and then whacked it on the edge of her desk. Holding the fork to her ear, she nodded us into song.

"Hail, Queen of heav'n . . ."

15

THE RED MOTORCAR

Sister Claire, my Second Babies teacher, was very tall, and her face, framed in its white wimple, was the face of a saint in a holy picture. When she moved, her veil moved, too, and it was like the black smoke from the chimney of the ship taking Aunt Kit back to England with her bike. Sister Claire sailed around the room all day like she had no feet, like she was a black swan on water.

On the first day of school after the summer holidays Sister Claire announced there would be a prize for the child who was best behaved and who didn't talk once during the day, except to answer her questions. She showed us how to put a finger across our lips to keep them sealed.

All day I kept my right elbow on the desk and my finger across my closed mouth. When I grew tired I put my two elbows on the desk. My nemesis, Paddy Connors, turned around in his seat and imitated me. Then he put his fingers up his nose, pulled his lips off his teeth, crossed his eyes, and made them nearly pop out.

Just before the end of the day, Sister Claire held up scissors and

two Friendly matchboxes as red and yellow as cowslips in the Limekiln Field.

The light glinted off the long legs of the spinning scissors as
Sister Claire cut and glued and stuck half of one matchbox on top
of the other one. She waved a piece of red paper at the children,
and in a flash the joined matchboxes had changed color. Then there
were white wheels between her fingers, and the matchboxes became
a shining motorcar. Sister Claire was a magician.

"This is the prize for the child who was best today," Sister Claire
said. She looked around the room.

I wanted to take my fingers from my mouth to say I had been the
best, that the other children had only been good while the motorcar
was being made. But I knew if I spoke I couldn't win the prize.

While Sister Claire scanned the classroom, my eyes started to
scald at the back because in my mind I knew I should be the winner.
But I would not cry. I would not give Paddy Connors a reason to call
me an oul girl.

Sister Claire turned sideways and sailed through the spaces
between the long desks to the back of the room, and I didn't think
I could keep the tears from bursting out. Paddy Connors looked
around again and stuck out his tongue and scrunched up his face.
He tickled himself under his own arms like Tarzan's chimpanzee and
laughed with no sound. He put one finger up his nose and another
across his mouth and pressed till his lips turned white. His were the
red eyes of the devil in the Penny Catechism. I was too unpracticed
in the ways of the world to know how to respond to Paddy's taunts;
all I could think of doing was putting him in the turnip pulper in our
boiler house and then mixing him into the mash for the sows.

"There was only one child who was good all day," Sister Claire
said, and I felt her hand on my shoulder. Then she stooped and put
the motorcar on the desk near my elbows. I got the faint and lovely
smell of roses as the edge of her veil touched my face. She put her

hand on my head and whispered, "You'll be a grand priest when you grow up, Tom."

I took the prize in my hands as if it were a day-old chick. The smoothness of the paper and the redness! Redder and shinier than haws and hips in the winter hedges.

This was one of the happiest things that had ever happened; it was as exciting as getting Aunt Teresa's birthday parcel from Dublin.

When the end-of-day prayers had been prayed, some of my classmates came over to examine the little car. When a girl reached out to touch it, I said, "You can only look."

"You can on-ly lo-ok," Paddy Connors said, imitating me. He reached out to grab my prize, and when I turned away he punched me in the back. But I wouldn't cry.

"You can on-ly lo-ok," he jeered again, making his voice sound high like a girl's. I dodged away through the desks and toward the classroom door where Sister Claire was saying goodbye to each child. She patted my head as I went by.

The second I got outside I held the motorcar close to my chest and ran like a hare. In my fear of the bully Paddy, I did not wait for my brother and sister.

Along the tarred road between the rows of houses on Harbour Street, I galloped until I came to our lane. Then I slipped around the corner of the Harbour Master's house, stopped, and peeped back. Even though there was no sign of Paddy, I turned and ran along the Canal Line, over Rourke's Bridge and up the Furry Hill, and then I saw Missus Fitz bent over in her garden in her long black dress and her grey war-stockings.

When Missus Fitz straightened up, she was all legs and wings like a heron stretching itself after standing all night on one leg in Rourke's Drain waiting for a minnow. She went up into the sky until the grey bun on top of her head was out of sight. Her face was the color of turf ashes. She did a little pantomime of holding her hand over her heart and gasping, "Mother of Mary, Tom Phelan! You nearly gave me a heart attack."

"Look what I won, Missus Fitz," I said, and I handed her the prize over the rabbit fence.

"Ah, Tom," she said, "and on your very first day back to school. Isn't it grand? I wonder where the nuns get such lovely paper." She held the motorcar at arm's length and made engine noises with her lips, drove the car around in a circle high above the flowers.

"I wish I had a motorcar like this," she said. "I'd drive to Dublin every day and go to the Fun Palace to see myself fat in the looking glasses." She drove the motorcar around in the air again and imitated the sound Malachy Quigley's tractor made three miles away on a frosty morning. The noise of the engine changed when the car went up and down hills and around corners. She made the horn squawk like the one in Doctor Duane's car, sounding like a duck halfway through swallowing a frog. She brought the prize car to a slow stop in front of my eyes. "Mind that motorcar now, child," she said. "Be careful when you're driving and don't crash into a cow."

As I trotted away I tried to make the sound of Doctor Duane's horn, but in the end I settled for *beep-beep*.

If I'd had a tail that afternoon, it would have been as lively as a lamb's at a milky teat.

16

TO SCHOOL WITH

UNCLE JACK AND RED

Like the Eskimos, who have learned to live in snow, the Irish have learned to live and work in rain in all its manifestations, except for one—"spilling" rain.

"It's spillin', lads."

Spilling rain, like bullets from machine guns, goes clean through overcoats, shirts, socks, and caps; it happens when God wrings out the black clouds and crashes his thunder to blast the piercing water from the skies.

My siblings and I walked to school every day unless it was spilling. On those days, Uncle Jack tackled and yoked the red pony to the cart in the shelter of the car shed. Red was bigger than our black pony, but where Black was a sedate female, Red had maintained the mind-set of an aggressive stallion who did not want to believe his equine jewels had been removed at an early age. Mam and the children drove Black; only Uncle Jack and Dad dared drive Red.

By the time we were ready to leave for school on a spilling morning, a thick layer of barley straw had been spread on the floor of the pony's cart. Amid a long duet of man-shouts and equine snorts and squeals, of threats manual and dental, Uncle Jack had enchained Red between the shafts, and in a state of high excitement, the pony trembled as he struggled to suppress the roiling energy confined beneath his red hide.

When we ran from the kitchen to the car shed, Uncle Jack was already outfitted against the weather. Standing in front of Red, he had an iron-fisted grip on each side of the pony's bit. Dad caught each of his children and flung us up over the wingboard into the straw. We lay flat with our feet to the rear of the cart; our schoolbags became our pillows. Two capes were spread over us. Then Dad took over the controlling of Red, and Uncle Jack sprang into the cart, settled himself on the seat, and clutched the reins in both hands. Finally, bending his head to avoid smacking it into the lintel, he signaled to Dad to step aside.

From the floor of the cart, I could not see Mam standing at the kitchen door. But I knew she was there, that she heard the wild neighing of our immortal steed, and that she gasped when thundering Red broke out of the darkness of the car shed into the shooting rain. I knew Mam moved back into the doorway when she heard the clattering of the iron-clad wheels as they bore her children out through the gates onto Laragh Lane. As the spinning wheels passed, she saw the charioteer with rubberized cape floating behind in the wind, girt around the temples with a sou'wester, leaning backward as he labored to restrain Red's fury.

I knew Mam was waving goodbye, saying, "I love you" in her wave, saying, "God bless you," and praying we would have a safe journey.

Lying in the soft golden straw beneath the bulletproof capes, I knew by the twists and turns and jolts where we were on Laragh Lane. I was in Cuchulain's war chariot in a cacophony of whipping chains and whacking metal-bound wheels, Uncle Jack's shouting, and the pounding of Red's iron-shod hooves. I was beside Cuchulain's charioteer, Laeg, lashing and yelling and driving with the speed of a swallow; I was a postilion clinging to the mane of the lead horse in a team of four, racing a ghostly, black hearse beneath a speeding moon in storm-ragged clouds, and driven by a flailing black phantom.

As Red sped off the lane onto smooth Harbour Street, I knew his iron shoes were blasting sparks out of the wet tarmac; I knew the chariot's wheels were leaving trails of fire behind them in the flowing surface of the road; I knew the earth was shaking and trembling with the velocity of our motion; and all the time the cart brayed and shrieked as the wheels of splashing iron went round, and strange cries and exclamations were heard in the air, as the ghosts of generations of Reds followed us.

I always felt safe because I knew Uncle Jack was in control of the reins, knew that Red could never beat him; knew that Uncle Jack, if the need arose, could bring Red to a shoe-and-hoof-melting stop within his own length. Uncle Jack was Hector, tamer of horses.

When we thundered past the rain-lashed, school-bound children on the footpaths, they turned to squint at the approaching fury, and put their terrified fingers to their mouths and pressed themselves against the fronts of the houses lining the street. The old people, wetly afoot, looked in amazement at this furious fairy-blast of noise, water, fire, and motion, and nodded to themselves in recognition of these descendants of the Tuah Dé Dana, who had arrived in mythical Ireland by way of magical whirlwinds.

17

ALTAR BOY DAYS

Learning the responses for the Latin mass was a time of warmth, love, and delight: warmth, because our group of eight potential altar boys sat outside on the steps of the sacristy in the autumn sun; delight, because I was being let in on the mysterious priestly language that rolled exotically around the tongue; and love, because I fell in love at age ten with the sweet voice, beautiful face, and slender soft fingers of Sister Carmel, the nun who was instructing us. No other part of her body was visible, and anyway I was too young to be interested in what was beneath her habit.

With her back against the black iron railing, Sister Carmel intoned, and eight voices eagerly repeated. The trace of a bemused smile put sparkles in Sister Carmel's eyes. Perhaps she was not used to dealing with boys of our age, or perhaps she was trying to keep from looking up our short trousers, our legs sprawled and spread; in those days only oul girls wore underwear.

"*Quia tu es, Deus, fortitudo mea . . .*" The lovely lips sent the words out sweetly into the air. Sister Carmel smelled like lilacs.

On the warm steps we almost sang the words she placed before us. When we had memorized the first page of responses, she recited the priest's lines, emphasizing the last syllable to wave us into our part.

"*Introibo ad altare Dei!*" I will go unto the altar of God.

"*Ad Deum qui laetificat juventutem meam!*" To God who gives joy to my youth.

The possession of the magical Latin words, the informality of the sunny setting, the feelings that Sister Carmel aroused, the mesmerizing sound of a group chanting a lesson by rote—all these created joyous moments. Before the instruction was over I was looking forward to the next one.

"Boys! Now that you are going to be serving mass you must always behave better than ordinary lads. You must give example by doing your homework and not getting into fights in school."

"Boys! You must always have a handkerchief in your pocket—no more using your sleeves."

"Boys! You may not serve mass with dirt under your nails or your hair not combed." I wondered who she was talking about until on the way home I noticed my filthy fingernails on the bike's handlebars.

As the lessons progressed during that autumn, not even the bully Paddy Connors's schoolyard jeering—"Cluck, cluck! Here comes the holy water hen!"—muddied my feelings of specialness, of being one of the chosen.

With the responses firmly embedded in our memories, we learned to genuflect in unison in the altar boys' sacristy: back straight, prayerful hands at chest, thumbs crossed, right knee landing beside left shoe, back straight when resuming standing position. If a boy lost his balance or bent over on the way down as if he had been kicked in the balls, we did the exercise over.

Learning to bow in one fluid movement was not easy.

"Boys! Bend your hips slightly, bring your shoulders forward slightly, and bow your head."

While I was inwardly gloating about the contortions of some of the others, Sister Carmel said, "It's hips, shoulders, and head, Tom

Phelan! You are doing shoulders, hips, and head, and if you try to bow that way you'll kill yourself."

Our first entrance from the priests' sacristy into the sanctuary was held in suspense as the nun tested, for the last time, each boy's Latin, genuflecting, and bowing. When she examined our nails, she bent down to my ear and whispered, "You have the fingernails of a priest."

"Boys! What kind of shoes must you wear to serve mass?"

"Black plimsolls, Sister."

"You carry the plimsolls from home to the sacristy, and then put them on here. Why must you wear plimsolls when you are serving mass?"

"So we won't be making noise like an oul farmer with hobnailed boots, Sister."

"And . . . ?"

"So we won't squash cow dung into the pictures in the floor, Sister."

"Mosaics!"

"Mosaics, Sister."

"What time must you be in the altar boys' sacristy?"

"Ten minutes before mass starts, Sister."

At last Sister Carmel opened the door of the priests' sacristy, and we got our first glimpse of the nave stretching away into the gloaming distance, hues from the stained glass windows hanging in the still air. I could see off to the Derryguile Corner, where men from that townland, kneeling on their caps with one knee and resting their leaning bodies on the other, congregated for Sunday mass. There, they gossiped and sometimes sold calves to each other, spitting on their hands before sealing the deal with a slapping of palms.

"Boys! You must be absolutely silent when you step onto the sanctuary floor."

In our socks we paraded like two rows of chicks following their black mother hen until we came to a stop in front of the enormous marble altar. Standing so close to it, I gasped at its height, its intricate carvings, and the angels and saints in their niches. The white of it!

In my excitement I did not see that the rear wall of the altar was undressed stone scarred with chisel marks. Nor did I notice then that in the space between the altar and the back wall of the church were stored the props used during the yearly liturgical cycle: the tall filigreed holder for the Easter candle, the folded Christmas crib, the purple penitential cloths of Lent, the six black candles used at funerals. In their untidiness, their symbolism was lost until nothing remained but pieces of wood and metal and cloth. This was the glamourless backstage of any theatre that is kept out of sight lest it spoil the illusions spun on the other side of the curtain. But I was seeing the church through the golden nimbus of youth and inexperience where there was no squalor.

Acting as both priest and conductor, Sister Carmel took us through the strict rubrical dance of assisting the celebrant of the mass. Every move and every step was choreographed.

"Boys! You must move so quietly, so smoothly, that only the priest is seen. You must become invisible to the people in the church."

We learned when to genuflect, when to stand, when to move the missal from one side of the altar to the other, when to bring the water and wine to the priest, when to strike the gong, when to bring water to the priest to purify his fingers, and when to get the paten to hold under communicants' chins. This last job turned out to be the best: sometimes a person's false teeth fell out, and to be holding the paten when the dentures came in for a landing gave an aura of specialness to the altar boy who caught them. And in the sacristy after mass, we would imitate the distorted features of certain parishioners when they stuck out their tongues for communion: the Tooth, Glass Eye, No Nose, Snake Tongue, and Tonsils. Their facial contortions became legend among generations of altar boys.

Eventually Sister Carmel was satisfied perfection had been reached, and with our heads full of liturgical Latin, we were altar boys at long last.

On the days when it was my turn to serve mass, I pedaled with delight along sun-brightened, dusty Laragh Lane that in fine summer weather was as different from the mucky lane of winter as sweetened tea is from castor oil. On mornings when tiny dewdrops glittered in the slanting sun, so many cobwebs on bushes and grass and weeds lit up that it seemed the whole world was tied down under a million strings of diamonds. In the joy and innocence of my youth I imagined the jewels had been strewn on the world by a happy and well-pleased God.

In my four years as an altar boy, I never once had the triumph of catching anyone's false teeth.

18

THE RECRUITER

One day a man dressed like a priest visited our classroom in the Boys School. But our teacher, Mister Sheehan, said the man was not a priest at all; he was a Christian Brother. I expected him to tell us an exciting story about some saint or martyr, maybe the one about Saint Lawrence roasting on a grill and instructing his torturers to turn him over so he would cook evenly, or the one about Saint Sebastian tied to a tree and getting shot to death with arrows. That's what I wanted to do to Paddy Connors.

If a person dies a martyr for the faith like Saint Lawrence, he goes straight up to heaven, like a woodquest shooting up out of a bush. If I died for Christ I would zoom right into heaven no matter what terrible sins I had committed. Even people who were not baptized, but who died for the faith, could be martyrs because their own blood would baptize them. It was better to die a happy martyr like Saint Lawrence on the grill than to die shouting curses at the lads cooking you because that was a sin against charity and then your place in heaven would be in the cheap seats far from God's throne.

Good health beamed off the Christian Brother. His black suit was without a speck of dirt; it looked new and fitted him like a glove. Beneath the suit was the body of a senior county footballer. His shoes were shining, with not even a daub of muck or dung on them. He spoke differently from the way we spoke; he sounded posh, and his lilt was pleasant to listen to.

"My name is Brother Conleth," he said, "and I am looking for a few good boys to join my religious order." Then he told us about a man from County Kilkenny, Edmund Rice, who founded the congregation of the Christian Brothers nearly one hundred and fifty years ago to educate poor children.

Brother Conleth said he was hoping to find a few hardworking, clever boys who could become famous like Edmund Rice. He talked about Saint Mary's College, the Christian Brothers school in Marino, in Dublin, where brothers in training lived manly and exciting lives and ate sausages for breakfast four times a week. Every boy there was given his own tennis racquet; the football and hurling pitches were as smooth as the tops of our desks, and nobody in Marino ever broke an ankle in a hole made by a cow's hoof. When the weather was bad, volleyball and badminton—games none of the students in the Boys School had ever heard of—were played indoors. Our education at Saint Mary's College would go all the way up to the H.Dip. and would be free. We would go to games in Croke Park. On warm, sunny days a bus would bring us to Howth Head to run up and down the grassy hills above the sea. And we would never be cold because the college had the most up-to-date central heating system.

Brother Conleth passed around large photos in which smiling and laughing boys were climbing ropes hanging from high ceilings, vaulting over gym horses, clambering up cargo nets, whacking speed bags while wearing real boxing gloves, diving into a swimming pool, and playing football and hurling in the sunshine. And there were photographs of boys dressed in the long cassocks priests wear. Brother Conleth said we would become teachers devoted to God and the saving of souls. "Your parents will be very proud to have a son in a religious order."

Before Brother Conleth had finished, all my prior priestly dreams collapsed into ashes—dreams of going on African missions dressed in a white cassock like the priests in the photos in *Far East* and preaching to smiling little pagan children with pearly white teeth, telling them how Christ died to save us from going to hell and burning in never-ending brimstone, and teaching them the times tables, too.

But now I decided to be a Christian Brother. I told Brother Conleth I wanted to go to Marino.

That evening Brother Conleth unexpectedly arrived in our farmyard. In the kitchen, he spoke to my parents, told them a God-sent vocation to the religious life should not be interfered with. He described the educational opportunities I would have in Marino, pointed out the social advantages they themselves would discover once they had a Christian Brother in the family.

The next day, after school, I changed into my damp work clothes and wellingtons. But I was dreaming of sunny Marino, where I would wear clean dry clothes and no longer have to slog through muck and mud.

Soon I was sitting on the seat of the pony's cart with Dad. We were crossing the pasture on our way to mend a fence. Just as I moved to get down to open the Bog Field gate, Dad stopped me.

"Tom, do you know those lads who come from Dublin to the Fair Day every month to sell stuff—the lads with penknives, tin openers, kitchen knives and forks and spoons, scissors? They stand up on a box and tell everyone how great their yokes are. The lad with the penknives claims they're made with steel that fell out of the sky a million years ago and landed in Germany and the blade never has to be sharpened."

I squirmed a bit on the seat. When I was ten I had bought one of those penknives against Dad's advice, and it fell apart after a few weeks.

"You'd think by the way the huckster talks, his penknives would cut stones and last forever. He will say anything to get people to buy the knives. But the knives break. The sharp edge lasts till you cut a twig."

Dad was staring at the wooden, tarred, barbed-wire-wrapped gate in front of us. I had never heard him speak for so long and I wondered why he was talking about the Fair Day hucksters. Maybe, I thought, he was going to give me a man's real penknife, one that I'd have all my life.

"Tom, that Brother Conleth is a bit like your man with the penknives. He goes around saying great things about the Christian Brothers to get young boys excited about going away to his school. And I suppose there are good things about the school. But he didn't tell you everything, the way the Fair Day hucksters don't tell you everything.

"Do you think if the huckster told you the blade will fall out of the knife in a few weeks that you would buy it? The Christian Brother didn't tell you you'll get homesick being away from your brothers and sisters and mother and father and your friends in school. He didn't tell you you'll have to get up at six o'clock every morning and wash in cold water and then make your own bed. He didn't tell you that every day you'll have to eat lumpy porridge for breakfast. He didn't tell you that whether it's warm or cold or rainy, you'll have to go out for a run every morning; that you'll be in a classroom from half eight to half twelve and then you'll have to eat whatever they give you at dinnertime whether you like it or not, and then you'll have to go back to school for another three hours. He didn't tell you that on Sundays you won't have Mammy's curranty cake or be able to go off across the fields with your brothers for hours or ride your bike to Tinnakill Castle. He didn't tell you that they harden up softies by letting the older lads teach them how to be tough. He didn't—"

"Dad, will you talk to him, tell him I don't want to be a Christian Brother after all?" I said.

"Sure, I'll tell him." Dad squeezed my shoulder. "Get down there now and open the gate like a good lad. We have a fence to mend."

BLESSED OLIVER

Every year on the Sunday closest to the feast day of Blessed Oliver Plunkett, Father McCluskey became an orator who grabbed his audience by the back of the neck and pushed its head into the blood and gore of the martyr on the Tyburn place of execution. Some parishioners had heard the sermon so many times that they mouthed the words along with the priest at the most memorable places.

Whenever I realized Father McCluskey was heading into the death throes of Oliver Plunkett, I listened anxiously, but assured, like a child knowing the outcome of an oft-told Jack the Giant Killer story at bedtime.

"Queen Elizabeth the first was the greatest heretic in the world. She was so cruel to Catholics in Ireland that when she was dying she armed herself with a red hot poker to fight off the devil, who had come to take her soul to hell. Three hundred and fifty years later she is still there and she will be there for all eternity. It's what she deserves. Blessed Oliver Plunkett may not have been martyred until eighty years after Elizabeth was dragged down to the depths, but it was because of the laws that great heretic made that he was martyred in the way he was.

"The English stole everything from the Irish for eight hundred years; they banned education, outlawed the Catholic Church, and paid rewards for the heads of priests, just like the Irish government pays a reward for a dead fox. When a priest was captured, hot pitch was poured over his head. When the pitch cooled, it was ripped off, and the priest's skin and ears and lips and hair came off with it. Sometimes, turpentine was poured over the priest's pitch cap and set afire. Then the priest was let loose to run all over the place like a human torch until he collapsed and died. Only the English could have invented punishments as cruel as pitch capping for the Irish and scalping for the Red Indians in America. But pitch capping wasn't good enough when it came to Blessed Oliver Plunkett. Oh no! He was the archbishop of Armagh and primate of all Ireland, Catholic Ireland's first citizen."

Every time Father McCluskey mentioned pitch capping, I touched my ears and lips.

"The English thought Archbishop Plunkett was becoming too popular and that he might get around to leading a rebellion, with all the Catholics in Ireland following him. So the heathens arrested him in Armagh and took him to Westminster to try him because they couldn't find witnesses in Ireland. He was found guilty of treason because by law that allowed the English to hang, draw, and quarter traitors at Tyburn. Drawing was like your mother pulling the intestines out of the Christmas turkey, only Blessed Oliver was alive when that was done to him."

I leaned forward and hugged my stomach.

"The English were barbarians who talked like they had harelips. That's why so many Irish place names were corrupted, like Carlow for Ceatharlach and Dublin for Dubh Linn. They took the music out of those names; they were a herd of buffalo grazing everything good out of the earth and leaving nothing behind except their dung."

I had never heard dung mentioned in church before. I wondered if Father McCluskey would have to go to confession.

"When Blessed Oliver was brought up onto the scaffold for execution, he forgave all those who had told lies about him, and those who were about to kill him. Then the Protestant butchers started in on him. First, they ripped all his clothes off and made him stand naked in front of the laughing mob. They tied his hands behind his back and put a rope around his neck. They threw the rope over a beam and pulled it until his feet were off the ground. Then they swung him back and forth to each other across the scaffold like he was the pendulum of a clock. The crowd of heretics looking on joined arms, and swayed with every swing, and sang 'See-saw, Margery Daw.'"

If I had been Blessed Oliver Plunkett I would not have forgiven the people who were going to cut me to bits, and from the tone of Father McCluskey's voice, I knew he would not have forgiven them either.

"When Blessed Oliver was nearly dead the executioner shouted out, "Behold the twitching bishop," and the people roared. The executioner teased them by twisting Blessed Oliver around and around and letting him spin like a child's toy. At last he was dropped to the floor with a bang and he collapsed onto the boards. They took the rope off his neck, dragged him over to the torture table, and threw him up on it like a side of bacon. The table was on a steep slope so that all the jeering heretics could see what was going on. Buckets of water were splashed over the bishop until he was revived."

I thought about the pig Dad killed each year and how I helped with the rubbing in of the salt. I hated the feel of the cold, dead flesh.

"The Protestant executioner stepped forward to the edge of the scaffold, held his sharp knife over Blessed Oliver's body, twirled it, and threw it up in the air. Then he spun around on his toes and caught the shining blade as it fell. The crowd screamed for him to start the butchering, but he kept on with his tricks; he dropped the knife onto his feet and then made it spring into the air above his head;

he twirled around again and this time caught the blade in his teeth. The crowd bawled like cattle for him to use it on the archbishop. The executioner danced back to the torture table and pretended to stab Blessed Oliver, but kept pulling back at the last second. The heretics squealed like pigs smelling food."

I wanted to shout, "Say it! Say what he did with the knife!" But as soon as he said it, my hands dropped to my crotch.

"The executioner grabbed the archbishop's private parts and with one quick slash sliced them off. He held them over his head and the crowd went delirious with delight. Then he flung the private parts out to the savages and they fought over them. The executioner spun his bloody knife again and the cries of the crowd became roars. He plunged the blade into the bishop's belly and sliced it open from chest to crotch.

"An assistant ran over, sank his hand into the open stomach and grabbed the end of the intestines. He walked backward across the scaffold while another man yanked out the guts. Then the two men started swinging the long piece of purple intestine like it was a rope. The executioner stepped into the rope and did all kinds of fancy skipping, the knife spinning up into the air and sprinkling the sacred blood of the martyr all over the place. The crowd—men and women and spiteful little Protestant children—cheered. An Englishman poured water on the archbishop to keep him conscious enough to feel the terrible pain, and another man pressed a dirty rag between Blessed Oliver's legs to slow down the bleeding and keep him alive as long as possible. The executioner stopped skipping and bowed to the audience while one of his assistants wrapped the intestinal rope around a stick to sell as souvenirs for a penny an inch."

Oliver's purple guts were the same color as the guts of our slaughtered pig slipping down into the galvanized tub we used for baths on Saturday nights.

"The executioner went back to Blessed Oliver. One after the other, with his bare hands, he ripped out the kidneys and liver and

spleen and pancreas and threw them into the crowd of hungry Protestant dogs. Then he dug his hand into Blessed Oliver's chest and
yanked out that noble heart, that still-beating Catholic heart. That
brave heart was held high for all to see.

"As slowly as they could, the savages on the scaffold chopped off
Blessed Oliver's legs and arms and then the head, the crowd making
a *hupp* sound with every fall of the axe. The head was put on display
on a spike at the Tower of London, but some brave Catholics stole it
and secretly brought it back to Ireland.

"God showed how wicked the English are, and how right Irish
Catholics are, by preserving Blessed Oliver's head and not letting the
flesh rot off it. His holy head is now in a glass case in Saint Peter's
Church in Drogheda, and after all these centuries the hair still grows
on it. Every Irishman and Irishwoman should visit that sacred head
and kneel and pray in Irish to show their Irishness and to remember
that the English are savages. *A n-anamacha leis an diabhal!* May the
devil take their souls!"

The sermon was finally over. I sank back in the pew as if I had
just run a hundred miles. Then, from the Derryguile Corner of the
church, Durt Donovan was heard to say, "Jazus, lads, wasn't it a good
job they didn't save Blessed Oliver's arse?"

20

THE SWEET PAPER

"Tom Phelan, say the Tenth Commandment."

"Thou shalt not covet thy neighbor's goods, sir."

"Neighbors" to my childish brain meant the people who lived on Laragh Lane, so this commandment was easy to obey. None of them had a radio, Aladdin lamp, gramophone, or fourteen piglets slobbering at their mother's milky teats; nor did they have a shed full of dry turf as winter approached. There were rumors that Durt Donovan had bags of money, but if he did, I wondered why he dressed like a tinker and was as dirty as a dog that has rolled around in another dog's dung.

If God had warned us that envy can land a person in trouble, instead of just telling us it's a sin, he might have saved me from lasting embarrassment when I was in third class.

Paddy Connors was one of the occupants of the two-seater desk in front of me. On a hot June day, when many townies had come to school in their bare feet, I saw Connors surreptitiously removing a toffee sweet from its wrapping and slipping it into his mouth. The sweet had softened in his pocket and the thin shape of the square was imprinted in toffee on the paper. When he threw the wrapper on the floor it landed toffee side up. Covetousness grasped me in her slimy, scaly tentacles, and I soon developed an all-consuming desire for that thin outline of toffee. I sank down in my seat, put my heel on the wrapper, and pulled it toward me. Then I picked it up, licked it quickly, and dropped it. Before it hit the floor, Paddy Connors raised his hand to get the teacher's attention.

"Mister Sheehan," he said, "there was a sweet paper under my desk and Tom Phelan just took it and licked it and I had stepped on it and there's cow dung on my foot. He might get sick, sir, and vomit."

"Is that true, Tom?"

"No, sir."

"He did so, sir," Paddy insisted. Then he bent down, retrieved the wrapper, and held it over his head.

"Did anyone else see Tom Phelan licking the paper?" Mister Sheehan asked. Several hands shot into the air.

I knew I had been caught in a lie. With his cane, the teacher instilled virtue by giving me six of his hardest whacks, three on each hand. The burning pain in my fingers and palms was gone by the end of the day, but the chant that followed me in the schoolyard and on the way home—"Rich oul farmers eat cow dung! Rich oul farmers eat cow dung!"—lasted until the jeerers' paths and mine parted at the top of Lord Edward Street.

21

SHERIFF JOHNNY'S GUN

Johnny Canning and I shared the same desk in Mister Sheehan's classroom. He was the nearest thing to a friend I had among the townies; at least he didn't say rotten things about oul farmers or push me for no reason whenever he passed me. I sometimes gave him a piece of Mam's curranty cake.

One day Johnny came to school with a silver-coated, ivory-handled cowboy gun and its leather holster in his schoolbag. Pinning on his lawman's badge at lunchtime he strapped on his weapon and strode around the playing field practicing his fast draw and shooting people. Boys of all ages, especially ones from the countryside like me, crowded around begging to pull the trigger.

"Ah, go on Johnny. Let me try it."

But Sheriff Johnny was a careful protector of his peacemaker, as he called it. "Mah name is Randolph Scott and this here is mah Colt .45, the fastest gun in the West. Don't touch mah weapon or ah'll drop ya. . . . Stand back or ah'll drill anyone makes a move," he drawled in his best Wyoming accent, and he quickly fired two shots into the crowd. A young country boy cried out in fright and Paddy

Connors shouted, "Kill them all, Johnny! They're all sodbusters putting up barbed wire to keep out our cattle."

"You don't even have a sheepdog, Connors," I said, and Paddy
knocked me onto my back, straddled me, knelt on my arms, and
kneaded my nose into my face; all snot and spit, I twisted away from
his torturing hand.

"Next time I'll rip your balls off, Phelan," Paddy said as he stood
up, and to prove he could do it, he ran his hand up the leg of my short
trousers and yanked down on whatever he found.

As Paddy turned away I jumped up and punched him in the
middle of the back. He fell. I took off and sped around the corner
of the ball alley. It wasn't long until I heard Paddy coming after me
shouting, "I'll kill you, you fuckin' farmer."

As I rounded the corner at the low end of the alley Paddy was
getting closer. Up ahead, Johnny Canning was still shooting and killing the bad guys. "Lie down! You're dead, you old cow puncher."

Paddy called out to his townie followers. "Make a posse! Stop
d'oul farmer, lads. Stop the bushwhacker."

The posse rode out from the gun-slinging action and pounced
on me, and just as Paddy fell down on me, Mister Sheehan shook
the hand bell on the steps of our classroom. But Paddy got in a few
smacks and face-slaps before he stood up. "Only a coward hits from
behind," he said, and he put his fist in my guts to lever himself up.

Everyone ran to the teacher's bell but Johnny Canning and I
stayed behind, he removing his holster and hiding the gun in his
waistband, I putting my disheveled self back together. Before we got
to our classroom, I had persuaded him to swap his six-shooter for the
telescope I got from Aunt Teresa for my birthday. "Look, it's made of
brass and it once belonged to a pirate."

The next day Johnny asked me to return the gun. "My uncle
brought it from England and if you don't give it back my father will
kill me."

"A swap is a swap," I said.

Ownership of that gun was so consuming that for weeks Paddy Connors, acting as Johnny's deputy, ambushed me, kicked me, beat me, pulled my scrotum, squashed my nose, and called me a crook to persuade me to hand it over. But I never did.

Even after the spring mechanism broke, I still used the gun to kill my brothers as we shot it out between the ricks in the haggard. With my six-shooter in hand, I was a white hat behind a rock in Arizona where the sun was shining and I always won.

22

MY BOXING CAREER

Father Flood, one of two curates in the parish, was as friendly and happy as a spinster's spaniel. Gentleness beamed eternal out of the round pale face haloed by a generous surround of white hair. He remembered everyone's name and chatted with Protestants as if they were Catholics. He did not play golf. Everyone said, "Sure, he's just like one of ourselves, so he is." And yet, in what seemed to be against the nature of the man, he founded a boxing club for the boys of Mountmellick.

Dad thought the club was a great idea. "You have to join, Tom. It'll make a man of you," he said.

I was eleven and I had come home from school many times in tears after bloody encounters with town boys. It had not yet occurred to me that on most occasions, I had brought the rage of the townies down on my own head by backing myself into corners with big-mouthed talk and scurrilous name-calling that could only be defeated with fists and boots.

Dad's first cousin, Paddy Horan, had once been the all-Ireland middleweight boxing champion. But twenty years later, when he returned home from "working on the buildings" in London, he was in no shape to climb back into the ring.

In Smith's butcher shop in the town, Don Tynan, in his blue-and-white-striped apron, chopped and weighed meat for customers all day. Tynan was young enough to still be boxing in local tournaments, and so he sometimes turned up to work with black eyes and a swollen nose. Until his wounds healed, Don was subjected to the smiles and comments of his customers.

"I see d'ass kicked you again, Don."

"Rasslin' with the wife again, Don?"

"Castrating another bull, Don?"

Don's reply was always the same. "You should have seen the other lad; mincemeat his face looked like, so it did."

For the opening night of the boxing club, Father Flood persuaded Paddy Horan and Don Tynan to give a demonstration match. There was no referee. There was no ring except for the circle formed by the boys in the middle of the upstairs floor of the Town Hall. Several townspeople also turned out to see the battle of the local Titans.

Paddy Horan, trailing his withered glory, was decked out in gallused trousers, old shirt, Sunday shoes, and boxing gloves; he was five feet seven inches tall. Don Tynan, ambitious to flatten a former champ, was dressed in above-the-knee shorts, maroon singlet, black socks, and canvas shoes; he was six foot one.

When they walked into the circle of boys they smiled at each other and touched gloves. Instantly, they began beating the living daylights out of each other. They were like two gamecocks fighting because it was in their nature to fight.

I sidled my way to the outside row of spectators. This wasn't sport. This was total war. This was the savagery of savages. This wouldn't be over until someone was dead.

Hatred and pain glistened in the cruel eyes of the boxers like a boy's eyes shine when he's getting six furious wallops on the hand from a stick-wielding teacher. With sweating faces as ugly as blisters on a larch tree, each man sent murderous punches into the other's upper body. They beat each other around the head, crushed each other's ears. Some punches caused knees to buckle. When one boxer staggered backward, the other followed and launched as many merciless blows as he could before the other recovered. Horan landed a nose-breaker on Tynan's face. Blood sluiced down the victim's philtrum, ran over his top teeth, and dripped off his chin, but despite his faltering knees and spurting blood, Tynan made a lightning recovery, and with a twisting, swiping punch he sliced open Horan's left eyebrow.

"Stop!" an angry voice shouted. "There was an agreement—"

"It was an accident," Paddy Horan gasped.

"Accident, me arse!" Tynan shouted.

Other big men ran in between Horan and Tynan and the gladiators were shuffled toward the door, one holding a sopping red handkerchief to his nose, the other trying to squeeze the gash in his eyebrow with his bare bloody fingers, the blood running down his arm to his elbow and then dripping onto the floor.

To the sounds of the boxers' shouting and heavy steps descending the stairs, the boys pointed in awe at the globs of blood blooming on the floor. As I gazed at the gore, I knew in my heart I did not want to be a boxer.

Dad was adamant that I belong to the club. "You have to learn how to fight off the townies when they go after you. As well as that, Mam has made you togs and dyed a vest maroon for you. And she ordered a pair of plimsolls in Shaws shop today."

"I won't get into trouble with the townies anymore, Dad . . . and it'll be too dark when I'm coming home from the boxing club—"

"Your brother can go with you."

And so, the following week, like Shakespeare's schoolboy creeping like a snail unwillingly to school, I walked the mile to the Town Hall accompanied by my little brother. The wooden stairs to the second floor were the steps to a mile-high gallows. As I dragged myself up, other would-be boxers flitted past me like moths flying straight to a flame.

I was wearing my shorts and vest under my clothes, and all I had to do was shed my outer layers. I was the only boy dressed like a boxer.

At that time, the Italian boxer Primo Carnera was still remembered as a heavyweight champion, and when Paddy Connors saw me tying on my plimsolls he shouted, "Put them up, Carnera! Look at Carnera's muscles, lads!"

My biceps were like knots on white thread. All the other boys gave a cheer, but there was jeer in it.

The club had no punching bags or workout accoutrements of a boxing gym. I ran with the other boxers around the perimeter of the room several times. When the warmup was over, we queued up for our first assessment by the trainers.

"Keep your head down and your gloves up," the trainer commanded, and I tried to take the stance of a champion. When he asked me to punch an imaginary face and shuffle at the same time, the trainer quickly saw I had not the makings of a champion. Paddy Connors was instructed to hit me in the midriff to see how well I would hold up to a punch. I doubled over in pain, squeezing tears back into their ducts.

I was relegated to holding up my gloved hands to the smaller boxers so they could practice their punches. The first one hit so hard that my own glove banged into my face. My nose bled.

Meanwhile, Paddy Connors quickly established himself as the best fighter in his weight group.

Excitement soared in the club one night when Father Flood announced he had arranged a boxing match between Mountmellick and a team in Kilkenny. The trainers had already chosen the members for our team, and everyone who belonged to the club would be brought by car to the match. In those days, Kilkenny was as distant from Mountmellick as Hong Kong is now.

When the day of the match arrived I set out alone for the Town Hall. Dad intercepted me at the wicket door and told me to bring my boxing outfit; in case some member of the team couldn't go, I would be able to replace him. Immediately Paddy Connors loomed in my imagination. He would crucify me if he found out I had brought my togs "just in case."

Dad was unable to hear my pleas not to make me bring my gear, and so holding a brown paper bag, I arrived at the Town Hall. About twenty boys reeking of nervous excitement milled around on the footpath as they waited for the cars to arrive. There was jostling and pushing and name-calling. Some of the boys pretended to be world champions and danced around with their fists up, their heads down, throwing punches into the air and snorting like young bulls meeting a receptive cow.

Paddy Connors stood in front of me.

"What's in the bag, Carnera?" Silence descended on the sidewalk.

"Nothing." I moved the bag behind my thigh.

"I never saw nothing. Let me look."

"No."

"I want to look at nothing."

A boy standing behind me snatched the bag from my fingers and threw it over my head into Paddy Connors's arms. Connors took out my shorts and dyed vest and plimsolls.

"Look!" He raised the trophies over his head. "Look! Carnera thinks he's going to be the champion tonight, but he can't fight his way out of a paper bag." Then he threw my clothes up into the air, shouted, "Carnera is the champion!"

The rest of the boys took up the chant and each time I bent down to pick up my gear someone dashed in and kicked it away. My plimsolls were thrown up onto a second-floor windowsill. The vest and the shorts ended up under Connors's feet. When I tried to push him off them, he knocked me down.

Connors was the only member of our team to win his bout with Kilkenny that night. I had silently hoped his opponent would flatten him, knock him unconscious, kill him.

The boxing match lasted so long that it was two in the morning when we got back to the Town Hall in Mountmellick. Dad had been waiting since midnight to bring me home. As we traveled along the Canal Line, me on the bar of his bike, I tearfully told him about the troubles the brown bag had caused.

"Would you like to give up the boxing, Tom?" Dad asked.

That night Dad was Saint George on a high bike.

23

TYRANNY OF THE
IRISH WEATHER

The weather exercised a tyranny over Dad's farming life, creating alternating periods of crisis and calm, and sometimes days of frantic intensity. The daily condition of the soil was ever present in my mind from the moment I could worry; if I was not working the soil first-hand, I was immersed in it by way of Dad's moods, which reflected the wetness or dryness, the workability or unworkability of our fields. But even during the occasional weeks of continuous sunshine, Dad's mood never soared, never became playful. No matter how warm the sun, no matter how dry the soil, in his mind there were always heavy-bellied rain clouds lurking behind Slieve Bloom, waiting to rise up and turn the earth into a quagmire.

For Dad, sunshine was not a gift; it was paid for many times over by months of slogging in boot-sucking clay. Staying one step ahead of the bills demanded constant and sometimes superhuman effort in whatever weather God sent. The hard work ruled out everything that was not necessary to the immediate task at hand. For Dad, the incessant labor dispelled all illusions, all dreams of an easier life. The only time his imagination took flight was when he wished aloud for specific misfortunes to befall his perceived enemies, chief of whom was Prime Minister Eamon de Valera. "That bastard!"

There was no escape from the soil, from a land prone to holding water. The soil became sloppy after even a passing shower, so its cultivation required immediate and Herculean efforts once the sun and wind had done their part.

Whenever Dad heard his children fantasizing aloud—"Wouldn't it be great to live in Arizona, where the sun shines all day?"—he collapsed their card houses with a cold breath of reality. Only work considerations counted; the spiritual and intellectual did not. Keeping one step ahead of the always offensive enemy ruled out idealism. All that mattered was creating tactics to get some fieldwork done on days when all four seasons seemed to repeat themselves in quick succession. This required a mind-set so ironbound that it was dangerous even to talk within Dad's hearing when he was working. What made his life all the more hellish was the Church's admonishment to accept the will of God, when he knew that the God who sent down all this misery from heaven was a mean and rotten bastard.

He was often gaunt with fatigue, and when he was under the pressure of weather-created anxiety, he sometimes slipped over the edge into extreme impatience. And sometimes he slipped over the precipice into a blind rage. He ruptured several relationships when he flared over a minor detail, like being charged a halfpenny too much for a gallon of paraffin oil. Whenever his anger began to leak out onto his children, it was Mam, by touch or look or word, who calmed him down. But Mam was not there to save me when the searing lava of his anger erupted onto me when I was seven.

The bad weather in the autumn of 1947 brought the farmers of Ireland to their knees as they strove to save their crops. Men and women and children spent long, slogging days carrying scythed cereal out of flooded fields, one sheaf at a time. Acres of potatoes rotted in the liquid clay. Mud and muck oozed into boots and crept up clothing to crotches and armpits. Despair hung in the low-slung clouds. The workers' fatigue doomed many fields of crops to abandonment. And all the while during those months of struggle, the turf that had been cut in the spring was being battered back into bog by the unceasing rain. There was no chance that our winter's fuel could be saved. Timber would have to be cut out of hedges, drawn home by way of horse-and-cart to be sawed and chopped. "Spare the sticks" would be the cautionary cry until autumn of the following year.

In our turf shed in October 1947 was a small pile of the previous year's turf that would last another month if it was used sparingly. When turf is stored, a wall of sods is built on the face of the pile to keep the turf tidy and reduce wastage. Our remaining supply that autumn stood only about a foot high, three feet deep, and five feet long, and so the preciousness of every tiny piece of the dwindling turf had been repeatedly drilled into us.

One Saturday afternoon Dad sloshed into the kitchen for a mug of tea. Everything about him was wet. We knew, as children can know, that this was not a time to play or laugh out loud. When Dad told my brother Eddie to put on his coat and cap and bring in a basket of turf, I volunteered to help so that I might escape the thorny atmosphere. I quickly dressed for the rain and ran out to the turf shed, where I decided to surprise my brother by jumping up on the clamp of turf and dancing a hornpipe. But it wasn't Eddie who came. It was Dad.

I still remember the beating he gave me, the whacking with the hard hands. I can still recall the feeling of utter rejection, of being thrown out of the shed and Dad's life into the heavy rain. I can still see myself in the farmyard in the rain, dancing in terror.

In our kitchen, a narrow and shallow alcove beside the big hob was where the floor brush was stored. For many years after the beating the alcove was called "Tom's Corner" because I made it my niche. When I sat on the floor and squeezed myself in, no one could get at me. When I pulled my knees up to my chest I was out of everyone's way. I was invisible. Into this cave I retreated to repair my hurt feelings, and there I discovered that hurt feelings, like physical bruises, need time to heal.

A long time ago, I stopped crying for the small boy I was then, but I still weep for Dad having to endure forever the remembrance of what he had done to me. I rue the fact that neither he nor I developed the communication skills that would have allowed us to talk about the incident, to hear each other's words of forgiveness.

Now, as an old man, much older than Dad was on that painful afternoon, I remember him as a man who loved his wife and his children, who at times was driven over the edge while trying desperately to provide for them.

24

DE VALERA AND
DAD'S TURNIPS

I was ten years old when Eamon de Valera came to Mountmellick on a Saturday evening to stump for the Fianna Fáil candidates running for office in the Laois/Offaly constituency. Our parish priest, Father McCluskey, had been influential in arranging the great man's visit. Supposedly McCluskey had spent time in prison with de Valera after the Black and Tans discovered a revolver hidden in the priest's house.

In 1951, Dev, as most people called him, was still somewhat of a mythical figure. Even those who did not agree with his politics were worshipful of the rebel who had evaded the firing squad in Dublin after the rising of 1916 and who had later escaped from an English prison.

Weeks in advance, Mountmellick's streets were swept. Celebratory bunting crisscrossed the welcome route. Tricolors fluttering from telephone and electric poles were yeast to the excitement.

Dev's visit was as anticipated in some quarters as the second coming of Brian Boru. Plans were made to attend no matter what the cost. People would spill out onto the highways and byways and cycle for miles; they would come in their ass-carts and horse-carts; they would arrive packed together in the backs of lorries; they would tumble out of overfull cars, limp and hobble to the Square to see and hear and cheer their hero.

I asked Dad if I could go to see Dev, but he wouldn't allow it. I pleaded with him, said I would be the only boy in the National School who would not be there. But Dad was unbending. During the week before the big day I tried to change Dad's mind so many times that he finally shouted, "If you mention Dev one more time I'll give you a good clout!"

There was a backstory to Dad's adamancy.

When Dev became prime minister in 1932, he announced that he was stopping payments on a substantial debt owed to England. Dev might as well have shot his own country in the two feet, as well as in the head and the heart. A six-year economic war with London began. Exports to the Old Mother were stopped, and many Irish farmers were caught with their farms stocked with beef that now had no buyer. Dad had to sell off cattle for about one-twentieth of the normal market price. From then on, any time Dev's name was spoken in Dad's presence it was met with a snort of derision, followed by "Bastard!"

And so, on the evening Dev came to town, I was driving our pony while Dad guided the turnip seeder along the top of the newly opened drills in Jer Dunne's field. The pony did not need any directing until we reached the end of each drill; then she had to be turned around and steered into the next furrow. Any horseman as good as Dad would have been embarrassed to be seen needing assistance handling a single draught animal, but there was a high hedge between the field and the Commons Road.

In the sky there was not the tiniest cloud, and the sun was still high above Slieve Bloom even as eight o'clock rang out in the church tower a mile away. The sound of the walkers, the bikers, the donkey-and-carters, and the horse-and-carters on the road beside the field had stopped long ago. As the pony and Dad and I trudged in silence up and down the clay, I fought to keep myself from asking one last time to be allowed to go to the town. I was afraid Dad would shout out the shaming words he used when he believed I wasn't pulling my weight on the farm: "How do you think the food is put on the table, the clothes on your back, the boots on your feet? You must think everything falls out of the sky." And finally the words that always cut me to the liver: "You're nothing but lazy!"

As the tolls of the eight o'clock bell faded into the countryside, an amplified voice sounded out like the voice of a corncrake: it was here, it was there, it was an echo, it was everywhere. Then we heard an enormous roar that went on and on. I looked at Dad but he was absorbed in steering the seed barrow. A voice in the amplifier tried to be heard over the cheering. The voice stopped and waited for silence, then tried again. The cheering faded. Then Dev's voice filled the world.

I was overcome by the absolute necessity to be in the place where everyone else was, to be able to say in school on Monday morning that I had been there, that I had seen the great hero. There were tears in my eyes as I begged, "Please, Dad, can I go?"

"Whoa!" Dad shouted at the pony and brought her to a stop.

For a moment my heart soared.

Then Dad spoke. "Look at me, Tom. Look at me! De Valera won't sow our turnips. Now drive on."

◆§ 25 §◆

EARLY MORNING CATTLE DRIVE

The livestock fair in Portarlington was held on the first Friday of every month. Dad sometimes opted to sell his cattle in that fair instead of the one in Mountmellick because it attracted buyers from farther afield. But Portarlington was six miles from home, and getting livestock there on foot and hoof was a small-time military operation, even if we only brought a few animals.

The journey began at six in the morning. Dad commanded from the front while standing in the pony's cart, pulled by the complacent Black. The handlebars and front wheel of a bike hung over the back-board, and a bundle of hay covered the rest. My brother Eddie and I were two horseless cowboys, while Ned Hyland walked behind, swishing an ashplant to keep the cattle moving. Ned had begun working with Dad after Uncle Paulie was sent into exile because of his fondness for the drink.

Ned had arrived in our farmyard on his bike at a quarter to six while Dad was hitching the pony to the cart. "We're leaving in a few minutes," he said to Ned, a hint of reprimand in his voice.

"Fifteen," Ned said.

"You have to eat your breakfast."

"I'll be ready at six. Isn't that the time you said we're leaving?" I liked the way Ned could stand up to Dad.

Ned was eighteen when he began working on our farm. He was a big brother to all of us, a tall and quiet man who became highly embarrassed one day when, after missing a rat with the tines of a pitchfork, he blurted out, "Hure!" in Mam's presence. For my brother and me, Ned was an unsuspecting educator. As we toiled with him in the fields he told us the entire plot of the last picture he had seen, and he introduced us to town life and the funny nicknames some people had, like Mickey Pigshite and Turkey Toes and Yaller Mick. He told us the gossip that our parents believed was beyond our years, like when a neighbor murdered her brother and a dead infant was found buried on their farm. And he made us laugh about the funny things Dad said when there were no children around: "Where's the pitchfork?" Ned asked. "Up me arse," Dad replied.

As six o'clock was striking in the church tower, Ned emerged from our kitchen after his breakfast of boiled egg, Mam's brown bread, and mugs of tea. I followed Eddie out onto Laragh Lane, both of us armed with ashplants to steer our three cattle toward the town. Then Dad drove the pony-and-cart through the tall galvanized gate; the lowing bullocks came next, with Ned driving them on from behind. Before we got to the Back of Fitzes field, I heard Mam closing the farmyard gates, and that sound locked the cattle out into a world far away from the familiarity and comfort of the farm and the other animals. They were in terra incognita, wandering from one side of the lane to the other; stopping and stretching their necks to allow for morose and wailing moos. When they passed low hedges they gaped across the top of the bushes as if contemplating a leap to freedom.

When Dad pointed and shouted from his crow's nest, Eddie ran forward past the animals to keep them out of Missus Fitz's front yard and flower garden. When we eventually came to the end of the lane, the cattle were driven sharply to the right onto the Borness Road toward Portarlington. In the slanting morning sun the animals examined every weakness in the hedges as if looking for relief from the hard surface of the road. What high heels are to a woman's feet, a macadamed road is to an ungulate because it has to use its hoof tip to bear all of its weight; in soft ground the toes sink in and the weight is dispersed throughout the foot.

Side roads and open gates also offered the cattle escape routes. From the pony's cart Dad called out when he saw an opening ahead, and Eddie and I took turns running forward past the cattle to stand guard. When the animals had slouched by, we fell in with Ned walking behind them.

At last, we passed the cemetery and drove the cattle up the railway bridge at the edge of Portarlington. As we crested the bridge, a church bell rang out nine o'clock.

Dad had told us that if anyone in Portarlington asked where we lived we were to say, "Just past Lee Castle." If a jobber knew we would have to drive unsold cattle home again for six miles, he would have Dad by the scruff of the neck when it came to bargaining.

When we arrived at the Market Square several farmers had already gathered, their small herds separated from each other by flailing ashplants and loud shouting. Forced to stand against the walls of the surrounding buildings, the frightened animals attempted to escape whenever they saw the opportunity, but they usually slipped and fell in cow dung or urine, slapped their chins against the hard surface, and then were shouted back into place as they tried to regain their hooves. When the cattle turned their rear ends to the walls and divested themselves of shovelfuls of sloppy dung, the green shite slithered down the pebble dashing to the pavement. But when they faced the walls and relaxed their sphincters, geysers spewed out onto the street, the splashes bouncing like buckshot off the road and splattering the boots and lower legs of the bystanders.

Even to a child of a farmyard like myself, the confusion, mooing, shouting, and the nervousness of the animals was unsettling.

Once we had claimed a space, Dad undid the bundle of hay in the cart and fed some of it to the bullocks, who munched while Dad and I stood guard. Ned and Eddie brought the pony-and-cart to the yard at the back of a farmer's shop, where they tied Black to a post and gave her food and water. Then they left for home on the bike, Ned pedaling, Eddie on the bar.

One of my jobs at the fair was to eavesdrop on the farmers and jobbers arguing over the price of an animal. The information I brought back gave Dad some idea of what price he could ask for his bullocks.

When the buyers approached Dad, they opened the hostilities by disparaging the animals.

"God! They're a hungry-looking bunch."

"Will you look at them bags of bones!"

"You must have run out of grass months ago."

Dad hated cattle jobbers as intensely as he hated rats, but he could not afford to let his temper loose on them. So on this day, he managed the would-be buyers by ignoring their insults, only speaking to them when they asked his price.

"Are you buying?"

"I might be."

"Are you selling?"

"I might be . . . I might be selling the three of them together."

"Where you from?"

"Out near Lee Castle."

"The one in the middle doesn't look too good."

I was always surprised at Dad's dealing with jobbers. He simply didn't answer when they tried to put him on the defensive. When he stated his price and the buyer came back with a meaningless offer, Dad didn't even look at the man. He went through the motions of taking care of his animals, rubbing one of them on the calming spot beside the tail.

"Well?" the jobber asked.

Dad ignored the man, went to another animal, and put it at ease with his magic fingers. He kept at it until the haggler had raised his offer within bargaining distance of Dad's price. After that, the deal was reached rather quickly.

From Dad's struggle to keep a smile off his face I knew he believed that even if he hadn't beaten the jobber, the jobber had not beaten him either.

Days later, Dad would unleash his feelings, shouting, "Bloody bastards!" while swinging a billhook at the stem of a bush as if it were a jobber's neck.

26

THE EARLY LIVES OF PIGLETS

Between Dad's three sows and Alice Burns's eager boar, the pig-house beneath our loft was seldom empty. When Dad was out in the fields and I was doing my chores at my own pace instead of his, one of my distractions was to stand at the Dutch door of the pighouse and watch the current litter of piglets.

In their confined, straw-strewn space, they were as frolicsome as lambs on a grassy hillside in springtime. They danced and squealed and flapped their ears and bucked up their hindquarters and chased each other in gleeful and snorty exuberance. After a performance of some pig-game in the straw, they would assemble inside the door as a group, gazing up at me as if waiting for applause. It was obvious from their expressions, their cocked ears, their twitching snouts, and their joyful eyes that they had a sense of humor.

Pigs are clever and curious. But they sometimes carry their cleverness a little too far, protecting their babies from marauders by swallowing them. Pigs also have excellent manners; they use one corner of their house to dispose of their droppings, thus keeping their soft straw bedding and themselves clean. Urban dwellers believe pigs are dirty because "as dirty as a pig" is part of the lexicon handed down to them.

One of Dad's streams of income came by way of having three litters of piglets to sell every year. When the time was near for a sow to deliver, he placed a chair in the porcine maternity ward, the defensive chair serving the same purpose as a lion tamer's. He often warned us that sows become dangerous if they think their young are threatened.

When the sow stretched herself out on the straw and showed signs of imminent delivery, Dad sneaked into her house with a cardboard box. Silently, and with one hand grasping the chair, he knelt at the sow's rear end. Every time the sow grunted and sent forth a piglet looking like a glistening sausage, Dad picked it up and put it in the box. Once the entire litter had been born, but before the sow struggled to her feet to inspect her children, Dad escaped into the farmyard with his shivering collection.

Carrying his future income into the kitchen, he placed the box near the fire to keep the newborns warm.

"How many had she?" Mam asked.

"Twelve and a runt." There was always a runt.

"Thanks be to God," Mam said.

As the children fled to avoid the birthy smell and the imminent squealing of the piglets, Dad named one of the boys to stay and serve as his assistant.

Piglets are born with sharp teeth. While suckling, they sometimes bite their mother's teats and make her so sore she refuses to feed them. So, before they got to the sow for their first meal, Dad broke off the piglets' teeth with a pair of pliers. Sitting on a kitchen chair beside the pig box, he chose a piglet, placed it on the sack on his lap, opened its mouth, and snapped off its two front teeth at the gums. Beyond giving a sharp cry, the infants didn't seem to feel any subsequent pain. Before Dad put the gummy piglet back in the box, his assistant dabbed it with black shoe polish to show it had been to the dentist.

When the piglets were two months old, the males were subjected to another medical procedure: castration. Castration dulled
their aggressive temperament, prevented the impregnating of female
kin, and kept the meat tender.

One afternoon when I was eleven, Dad appointed Eddie and
me as his surgical assistants. Armed with his chair, Dad had already
evicted the sow from the pighouse. But instead of driving her out
into the pasture, well away from the operating theatre, he left her in
the farmyard. Then he tied the top half of the door to the wall to let
in the light.

While we were setting up for surgery the sow began poking the
lower door and snuffling suspiciously.

"Don't mind her," Dad said. He sat on his chair and spread a
burlap sack on his lap, transforming it into an operating table. In the
breast pocket of his jacket was his cut-throat razor, sharpened on a
roof slate dampened with oil. In his side pockets were a tin of boot
polish and a bottle of Jeyes Fluid.

The assistants herded the piglets into a corner. When Eddie
caught one by the back leg, it squealed piercingly, and immediately
the sow's two trotters and head appeared over the half door. Eddie
and I gaped at the threatening, slobbering, grunting head with its
large flopping ears, sniffing snout, and little red eyes.

"Don't mind her," Dad said again.

Keeping one eye on the sow, Eddie glanced at the piglet's rear
end and declared, "Girl!" I dabbed on a streak of polish and Eddie
released her.

The second captive was a boy. When it squealed, the murderous
snuffling of the sow at the door went up an octave.

Eddie placed the piglet on its back on Dad's lap and held its rear
legs apart. I held the front legs steady. The piglet screamed, the sow
shook the door, and Dad wielded the razor. He slit the barely bulging
scrotum, fingered out the testicles, cut their anchors, and flung them
over the sow's head and into the yard. The sow dropped off the door,

sniffed around until she found the delicacies, and then gobbled them up. By the time her head and trotters were back on the door, Dad had dripped some Jeyes Fluid on the surgical wound, I had applied the polish, and the piglet was back with its siblings, wondering what all the fuss had been about.

That day Dad performed seven surgeries and the sow feasted on seven hors d'oeuvres.

When we emerged from the operating room, Mam was standing at the kitchen door. Frowning and with reprimand in her voice, she said, "JohnJoe! I was standing here terrified the sow would break down the pighouse door." I had never heard Mam speak so strongly to Dad. But her children had been threatened along with the sow's.

Seamus Heaney in *The Early Purges* wrote, "'Prevention of cruelty' talk cuts ice in town, / but on well-run farms pests have to be kept down." City dwellers might think Dad's treatment of young pigs was savagely cruel; however, aside from the necessary physical intrusions, the piglets received tender and loving care in the warmth of their little house from the day they were born. When their mother's teats ran dry, they were put on a tasty diet of bran, pollard, cow's milk, and potatoes and grew plump and healthy.

When Dad was satisfied with the weight of the piglets, he prepared the pony's cart for their journey to the Portarlington pig fair. He stapled burlap sacks onto the creels; made a burlap roof, leaving a small space at the front for himself to stand up in; he spread an armful of soft barley straw over the floor; and stowed three waterproof capes in a corner of the cart to cover the piglets if it rained. This pony-pulled conveyance measured five feet long, three feet wide, and three feet high from the axle.

In the pighouse, Eddie and I grabbed each piglet by the tail, slipped an arm under its belly, lifted the animal, as wriggly as a fish on a hook, and held it close to our chests. The piglets sang ear-piercing arias while being removed from the only home they had ever known. Gently we placed them in the pony's cart.

Bringing the pigs to the fair was a two-person job; on arrival, Dad would bring the pony off to a stable, and I would stay at the cart to discourage pignapping. And so when the pigs had been loaded and before the rear creel was latched in place, I climbed in the cart and settled in a back corner in the straw. From the front of the cart, the piglets sniffed and twitched their curious snouts at the smell of my wellingtons and Uncle Jack's heavy topcoat, which I was wearing over my own. When they decided I was not a wolf in Uncle Jack's clothing, the pigs went about exploring their new quarters. Perhaps they were looking for the breakfast Dad had denied them to keep them from throwing up due to motion sickness.

Mam and all my siblings were at the kitchen door to wave us off into the big world with Dad's little harvest, Mam moving her lips in prayer for the safety of her men—and for a good price.

It was because of the black pony's easy gait that Dad used her to haul the pigs. When Black took her first step, all the pigs fell as the world beneath them moved. Unnerved, they piled into the corner beside me at the back of the cart, several of them stretched across my legs. It was only because I was wearing wellingtons that I endured the sharp-hoofed jabs of the ever-moving bodies.

I could not see through the protective sacking on the creels. Covered with piglets to the knees, I was relieved that I was hidden from the world; the town boys would be denied new fodder for their "dirty oul farmer" jeers. By the time we arrived in Portarlington, the piglets and I had been jogged to sleep.

During the selling process I discovered a side of Dad I had not known. When an abrasive middleman looked in at the piglets and said, "God, dem's terrible tin yokes altogether," Dad went right back at him.

"You don't look so good yourself, you gobshite. You wouldn't know a pig from a ferret. Feck off and don't come back."

By noon the piglets had been sold, and without any emotion we handed over the litter that had lived with us for three months.

The last mile of the road home ran parallel to Laragh Lane, a half-mile distant. Across the fields separating the Portarlington road from our lane floated the jangling of the draughts, the clattering of the wheels, the jingle of the britchen's two short chains, and the clip-clop of Black on the hard surface. Snug in my straw, I knew Mam would hear the unique music of our cart. Not only would she be glad for the safe return of her men, but she would also know by the lightness in the music that the cart was empty.

27

HORSES

On clear days when I went out with Dad to the Back of Fitzes field carrying a handful of crushed oats in a bucket, our horses trotted toward us no matter how far away they were grazing. At the last moment they played catch-me-if-you-can by turning and throwing their heels into the air, displaying their hindquarters, and sometimes sending out crackling farts. But the sound and smell of the oats quickly overcame their antics. When the horses dipped into the bucket we caught them by the forelocks and slipped the winkers over their heads.

It was an adventure catching the horses on a foggy morning. The grey walls shut out the world, and Dad and I were isolated in a huge igloo where the light was strange and sounds were muffled. Water-soaked grass, bent over with the weight of so many droplets, demanded the wearing of wellingtons.

Hidden in the fog, the horses played games of catch-me in the five acres of the Back of Fitzes. Dad and I stood in our igloo swishing the oats and listening for a snort or a plod, for any clue as to where the horses were.

"Bastards!" Dad said. Then he began to call, "Pyoh, pyoh, pyoh," and swished the oats in the bucket. *Pyoh* was an imitation of the sound of a horse's long upper lip vibrating. We listened. We walked farther out into the field. "Pyoh, pyoh, pyoh," Dad said, then added, "You call too, Tom." So I pyohed along with Dad as he shook the bucket.

"Bastards!"

Then thirty feet away, like the head of a dead deer on a rich man's wall, we saw Lame Mare's head hanging on the side of the igloo. Dad held out the bucket and pyohed. The mare backed away, then disappeared.

"Bastard!"

Even though Dad used his worst swear word on Lame Mare, he had special affection for her. He had once yoked her to a log that was heavier than he thought, and when she pulled she hurt herself. Ever since, she walked with a limp in her right hip. But despite her lameness she was a dedicated worker with a serene and patient personality.

Lame Mare's daughter, Whiteface, was a perpetual teenager, forever trying to get out of working hard, never pulling her weight in a team, always stopping to snatch a grassy mouthful on the headlands, always distracted, always more difficult to catch.

Our other horse, Timahoe, was not related to Lame Mare or her willful daughter. She was named after the local village where she was bought. Taller than the other two, she was black while the others were red.

Dad and I walked to the spot where Lame Mare had disappeared, but as the wall of the igloo moved away in front of us, there was no sign of her except the marks of her hooves in the sopping grass. We began to follow the hoof marks but had taken only a few steps when we heard a *pyoh* behind us. We turned and on the far wall saw her. Dad lifted handfuls of oats and let them drop noisily down into the bucket. We approached the mare in the foggy igloo, but we never seemed to get closer. She kept backing away from us.

"Bastard! She's playing."

Her head disappeared and behind us we heard a snort. White-face was hanging on the far wall. She pyohed and I glimpsed her long teeth through her vibrating lip. But then Timahoe spoiled the game by walking into the circle and sticking her head in the bucket. The others had no choice but to run in and claim their share of oats.

THE HORSES WERE an intimate part of our farming lives. For weeks each spring Dad spent his days holding the handles of the plough, the reins over one shoulder as he plodded behind the mares pulling the plough. Whenever I was the one to bring him his four-o'clock tea, I stayed to walk behind him in the fresh furrow made by the curving plough. The lifting of Dad's boots in front of me, the solid plodding of the horses, the nonstop turning over of the new sod smoothed by the plough's wing, the sailing of the seagulls, the cries of the small birds, and the shouts of the bigger ones following us to grab upturned worms, gave me the feeling of being immersed in Dad's world and circumstances.

Dad often repeated his rule about dealing with horses: "Never stand behind a horse's rear end or walk up to it." He had known a man who came up behind his horse, gave him an affectionate slap on the rump, and said "Hupp!", unknowingly frightening it. The horse lashed out with a hoof, hit the man in the stomach, and killed him.

At sugar beet harvest time, a notice arrived in the mail that a ten-ton train wagon would be available to Dad on a certain date to bring our crop to the factory. Ned and Dad loaded the cart from the roadside pile that had been drawn out of our field weeks before. Even though Timahoe was strong and fast, this enterprise required hard work of man and animal. The men loaded a ton of beet by way of eight-tined forks; Timahoe hauled the ton two miles to the train station, where the load was tipped onto the ground. Then, a hired man threw the sugar beet in over the side of the wagon, which was eight feet off the tracks.

No time could be lost. On one of his ten return trips from the station, Ned was trotting Timahoe one step short of a gallop when the horse stumbled and fell. Ned was thrown forward and sideways out of the cart, landing on all fours. As Timahoe struggled unaided to her feet, a woman passing by on her bike stopped and scolded the prostrate Ned. "You were running the horse too fast. Look at his knees; they are all skinned."

Ned held up his bleeding palms and said, "Fuck the horse! Look at my hands and knees."

I learned at an early age how to tackle the horses, even though at first I needed an adult to buckle the belts holding the collar and the hames in place around their necks. But I could lift, balance, and let the straddles fall onto their backs, then reach under their bellies and cinch the straps in their buckles. I loved tackling the horses. Being able to do so made me feel that I was appreciated by Dad, that I was an accepted part of the effort to wrest a living from the land, that I was "getting big."

In early spring a concrete roller was used in the grazing fields to level out the cattle hoof-holes from the previous autumn. I was ten when I was left alone in a field for the first time to work one of the mares at this job. At twelve, I was entrusted with two horses to spike-harrow and spring-grub the newly ploughed fields. Walking behind the horses through the freshly tilled clay I felt a palpable connection with the soil. The soft stirring of the soil beneath the teeth of the tilling implements was mesmerizing to eyes and ears. And there were the trailing, worm-seeking birds; the chirping finches; the cawing crows; and the shrill cries of the bullying seagulls. I remember the sinking of my feet into the fecund clay, the smell of the horses, and spring rising up out of the awakening earth filled me with a mysterious contentment.

I never rode any of Dad's mares. Neither did he. The only people I saw riding were properly rigged-out "rich" people on saddled horses, or tinkers galloping bareback and using raveling binder twine as reins. Perhaps Dad, not being properly equipped or else too proud to be associated with the tinker culture, chose not to be an equestrian. He did not encourage his children to ride either. The only time my siblings and I were on horseback was when Mam took a photo in the farmyard with her Brownie box camera. In the photograph, Dad is holding the horse, his anxiety for the precarious perch of his five children obvious on his face.

Because the horses were so valuable, the most regularly consulted tome in our house was an anatomy book with diagrams of equine bits and pieces. Dad took great care of his horses and regularly scraped out the hooves of his three mares. During the winter the horses were housed in the stable. Every morning, while Dad cleaned the stable and scattered soft barley straw, the children walked the horses around the farmyard for ten minutes and then brought them to the water tank.

In wintertime their bellies and sides were shorn to keep them clean when they lay down. Shearing was a job for a wet day or when it was dark, because Dad would not waste daylight or good weather doing it. The stable was a dark place, and without the yard lamp it was impossible to use the long-handled shears. The yard lamp, fueled with paraffin, had a flame inside a glass globe that provided slightly more light than a candle.

One night while Dad sheared I held the yard lamp close to the action. Why was I the one chosen to hold the lamp while my brothers and sisters were inside in the warm kitchen? I complained silently.

"Can't you shine where I'm clipping?" Dad said. How was it that no matter how I held the lamp, I was not lighting up the correct place?

Along through the red horsehair Dad's shears clip-clipped, leaving behind an oxford-grey, two-inch swath. But when impatient Dad pushed the shears too hard, creating a wave of hairy flesh that ran before the teeth until they eventually caught the flesh and pinched it, the mare then raised a hind leg and whacked her hoof on the floor. Dad slapped the horse's side with the shears. It was unlikely the shears hurt much, but even so, the slapping made the horse react by squashing Dad and me up against the wooden dividing wall. And so it went, until man and horse were very annoyed at each other.

"I'll put the touch on you!" Dad shouted as he smacked the mare in the ribs with the flat of his hand. The "touch," a rope noose on the end of a short stick, was used to render a mare immobile with the threat of severe pain. The upper lip was pulled through the noose, which was tightened by the twisting of the stick.

Silence on my part was the wisest course to take. Dad was a true believer in the catechism teaching that "animals were made for man's use and benefit." He never allowed an animal to win.

28

THE FORGE

Dad told us children, "If a big person ever asks you questions about the farm or about the cattle or the pigs or our family, just say, 'I don't know.' It's not telling lies. It's a way of telling him to mind his own business."

The place where we muttered the most "I don't know" answers was at Peetie Flanagan's forge. Peetie Flanagan was a big man with a hairy chest, unkempt hair, and giant hands that could have squeezed water out of a stone.

Besides shoeing horses, ponies, jennets, and donkeys, Peetie also made iron gates and drill harrows. His forge, a galvanized shack attached to the end wall of Laffey's bike shop, was a most untidy place, with bits and pieces of farm implements piled on the floor against the left-hand wall. Two of the shack's corners were so dark that monsters with metal teeth and eyes might have been crouching in them. Directly inside the open door was a space large enough to accommodate a horse. To the right side of this area stood the anvil, bolted to a block of wood studded willy-nilly with old horseshoe nails hammered in during idle moments. Beyond the anvil were the fire and the bellows. The doorway, the only source of light, also served as chimney for the smoke of the anthracite. Everything in the forge was black, everything coated with the fine residue of burned coal.

I loved being in the forge with its flying sparks, ringing hammers, wheezing bellows, and the foreign smell of anthracite. Being in the blacksmith's was to be among grown men who said "fuckin' dis" and "fuckin' dat."

When I was eleven our mare Timahoe needed new shoes, and Dad waited for a wet day to bring her to the forge. Eddie and I went along in the pony's cart, Eddie sitting backward holding the reins of the mare trotting behind.

Outside Peetie Flanagan's, droopy-hatted farmers were already standing in the rainy street, each with a naked horse, waiting their turn to go into the forge. Dad paid Peetie in advance and left us with instructions about leading the mare home through the town when the job was done. Before he climbed back into the pony's cart he whispered, "Them oul lads will be asking you all kinds of questions. You know what to say." We took our place at the end of the queue.

No sooner was Dad out of sight than a red-faced man who hadn't shaved in a week asked, "How many horses does your father have?"

My brother said, "I don't know."

"Be Janey! You don't know a little thing like that?"

When an animal relieved itself inside the forge, Peetie swept the effluvium out the door and across the footpath and built a dam with it in the gutter. In the puddle of rainwater and urine that formed behind the dung he cooled red-hot, newly forged shoes. Peetie himself carried them out with tongs and dropped them in, where they hissed and steamed and spluttered and threw drops onto the legs of his trousers.

The farmer ahead of us looked as if he had spent days standing out in the rain. The rim of his hat had collapsed and it looked like an upside-down flowerpot.

"Are you the one that's going to be the priest?" he asked me.

"I don't know."

"Well, everyone says you are."

A newly shod horse was led prancing out of the forge with his hooves shining. The owner shortened his grip on the reins and the horse whinnied loudly at the waiting mares. Peetie stood in his doorway in his leather apron and called, "I'd swear one of that lad's balls was left in when you cut him, Mick. There's too much spunk in him altogether."

Out of the spills of rain a waterlogged farmer led his water-logged horse into the forge. A man behind us tied his animal to a telephone pole and went inside out of the rain.

"One of us should go in, too," Eddie said. "It's no use the two of us getting wet. We'll take turns."

"We'll toss," I said. "I have a penny."

Eddie won. He went into the forge and I stayed outside holding Timahoe's reins.

"Hey, chappie! Does yer fadder still raise them little pigs?" a man called from the forge door.

"I don't know."

"Oh fuck off, you little sleeveen. You know fuckin' well."

It was the first time anyone told me to fuck off, and I felt as if I had been severely scolded.

A farmer behind me shouted, "Hey, young lad! You look like a rale Hayes, but you couldn't be one because none of them men ever got married. Is your mother a Hayes?"

"I don't know."

"You don't know your own mother's name? Are you an eejit or what?"

I felt like a fool. I began to wonder whether Dad's order to stay closemouthed was a wise one.

Finally it was time to lead Timahoe into the forge. Peetie and his apprentice, Pierce, pushed her into the best position for the light to brighten their work space. Before Peetie grabbed Timahoe's fetlock, I asked him if I could pull the bellows.

"Yes, but only when I tell you, and don't touch the fire or the iron in it."

The bellows was a monstrous contraption, operated by pulling a chain hanging from a pole attached to the top side of the blower. The real joy of blowing the burning anthracite was seeing the iron turning red and then white. The exotic smell of the burning coal and the heat from the fire on a chilly, wet day were wondrous, the beating of the rain on the galvanized roof adding another layer of comfort.

"Hey, Phelan," one of the waiting farmers said to my brother, "did your father sow sugar beet this year?"

"I don't know."

"He did," the blacksmith said as he dropped Timahoe's hoof. Peetie leaned against the mare's side. "He sowed three acres like myself, and I have the best beet I ever had. And I want you, young fella"—he pointed his pincers at me—"to tell your father I was drill-harrowing my beet on Monday, and my beet is so big the harrow got stuck between two of them and the horse was brought to a dead stop. What do you think of that, men?"

"Bejazus, Peetie."

"You must have put great dung in the drills."

When Peetie bent down to lift up Timahoe's hoof, the men winked at each other.

"Hey, Phelan, I heard your father's pony ran away in Marbra last Sunday and crashed into the back of a motorcar. Is that right?"

"I don't know."

"I don't know! I don't know!" the man sneered. "It'd be easier to get a fart out of a dead ass than get an answer out of you."

The men chuckled. One of them said, "I asked yer man on the bellows the name of his mother and he said he didn't know."

Peetie threw one of Timahoe's old shoes onto the pile in the dark corner. On his way to the mare's rear hooves he said, "She's a Hayes from up the road, sister of Paulie's and Billy's and Jack's."

"I knew he was a Hayes the minute I looked at him." Turning to me, he said, "I hope you don't grow into an old bollicks like your grandfather."

"He's going to be a priest," someone said.

"No better job . . . a motorcar and the best of grub and not having to work for it."

"Free house, too, and golf all day."

"Aye, and an oul one of a housekeeper to look after you."

"No temptation there, lads! Priests' housekeepers always look like the back of a bus."

Pierce, the apprentice, was wearing a sleeveless shirt and his biceps were big, bulging, and blue-veined. He wore a leather apron, too, to protect against the sparks flying from the hammer-whacked, white-hot iron. He swung the big sledge and flattened the iron while Peetie used a lighter hammer to shape it into a shoe on the points and edges of the anvil. Like the sound of a ticking clock the two hammers rang out an even staccato until an "Up!" from Peetie interrupted the flow. The blacksmith held the long-handled punch while Pierce whacked it to make the nail holes.

"Hey, Phelan . . . you holding the horse's head," a man said. "Was your father in Port fair with cows last Friday?"

"I don't know."

"What do you mean you don't know? Do you know anything at all? Do you know even what feckin' day it is?"

Peetie Flanagan was walking back to the anvil after dropping a horseshoe in the horse-water outside the door. "Ah, leave them lads alone," he said. "For all we know, JohnJoe told them not to be talking about things that do be going on at home."

"Is that right, chappie? Did your father tell you that?"

"Leave the chap alone," Peetie said. "Sure, we all have things we don't tell anyone. Like I never give away the price I get for an animal at the fair, and you'd never ask me and I'd never ask you either. Them lads are not old enough to know what should and shouldn't be talked about, so they don't talk about anything."

Peetie bent over, with his back toward the horse's head. He grabbed the fetlock, lifted the leg, and put it between his knees. Our Timahoe was a quiet mare, but even so, my brother kept a tight grip on her bit.

If any horse moved or tried to regain control of its leg while being shod, Peetie shouted at the farmer for not holding the horse steady. "Do you want me to get fuckin' kilt or what?"

It was also the farmer's fault if his horse nipped Peetie. "If this fucker was mine, he wouldn't bite a second time because he'd have no fuckin' teeth to bite with!"

Sometimes, while a horse's leg was still locked between his knees, Peetie gave the animal a punishing elbow in the stomach and snarled, "Hold up there, ya hure!"

"Do you have a name on your horse, chappie?" a farmer asked Eddie.

"Yes. Timahoe and she's a mare."

"Glory be to God on high, the lad knows something."

When the blacksmith and his helper finished making a shoe, Peetie inserted the point of his punch into one of the nail holes to make a handle, and he pushed the red-hot iron against the mare's hoof. Then he threw the shoe in the urine pool and took the new piece of glowing iron out of the anthracite and shaped it on the anvil. When the iron for Timahoe's third shoe was pushed into the glowing anthracite, Eddie took my place at the bellows.

Watching the blacksmith hammering the square-headed and sharp-pointed nails through the shoe holes and into the hoof, and then twisting the protruding ends off the nails between the claws of his hammer, was like seeing a circus clown perform a succession of tricks he has done ten thousand times. Silently, like a nurse anticipating a surgeon, Pierce was always one step ahead of the blacksmith's needs. He passed a heavy rasp to Peetie, who filed the nail edges and the hoof smooth; he handed Peetie a brush for painting the hoof with old engine oil out of a dented tin can.

When he finished the job, Peetie slapped Timahoe on the rump for being such a good client. Then he said, "Now, lads, there are seven nails in a horseshoe. Would it be cheaper for your father to pay me half a crown for each shoe with its seven nails, or one penny for the first nail, two pennies for the second, four for the third, and so on up to the twenty-eighth nail?

"The first way," Eddie and I replied in unison.

"Be gob, men," the blacksmith said, turning to the other customers, "these lads are not as thick as you'd think."

Peetie said, "Don't forget to tell your father about my drill harrow getting stuck between two beets."

When we told Dad this, he said, "Either Peetie is an eejit or his horse is worse than a bad ass."

WHITEFACE AND THE STALLION

Every afternoon at three o'clock, with my schoolbag strapped on my back and my kneesocks at my ankles, I was gushed out through the narrow schoolyard gate in a stream of escaping boys. One day when I was about twelve, I unexpectedly saw Dad at the Long Barn, sitting on the wooden seat of the pony's cart and waving to get my attention. Wearing his good grey hat with its black band, he had washed his wellingtons at the pump trough before leaving home. The hat and the sparkling boots stood in sharp contrast to his soiled workaday clothes.

Except for her winkers, the mare, Whiteface, was standing naked and somnolent behind the cart, her head hanging and her reins in Dad's right hand. With one foot on the box of the wheel and my hands gripping the wingboard, I vaulted into the bundle of straw behind Dad's seat; he greeting me by running his hand through my hair. Then he passed the mare's reins to me with the instruction, "Don't wrap them around your hands, Tom." This was to protect me against being dragged out of the cart if the mare suddenly stopped or shied. I shook the reins to get Whiteface's attention.

"Hold her, now," Dad said, and he dropped the pony's reins along her back and hupped her forward. Within a few seconds, he turned back to me and said, "We're going to trot, Tom. Hold her tight." And we set out on the clip-clopping six-mile journey to Marbra—a corruption of the regal Maryborough—where the mare had a date with a stallion in the yard behind Ramsbottom's shop.

Once we left Mountmellick behind, Dad unwrapped the butter-and-jam sandwich Mam had made for me. He took a bite for himself before handing it to me. Next he pulled the newspaper twist out of a lemonade bottle, took a long swig of sweetened tea, and then gave it to me. "If there's any left, I'll drink it."

Dad was addicted to tea. When he got up in the morning, he looked around for teacups containing dregs from the previous night, poured them into one vessel, and drank it cold. Then he lit the turf fire to boil the kettle. Whenever he spent the day working around the farmyard, he came into the kitchen for tea so often that Mam said, "It's a good job he doesn't drink porter!"

From Mountmellick to Marbra the paved road ran across a deep bog that stretched, heather-covered, to the horizon. For miles we saw neither animal nor human. Along the lonely road we trotted to the music of grinding iron-shod wheels, the jangle of the pony's tacklings, the jingle of the draughts, the light rhythm of the pony's hooves and the heavier one of the mare's hooves smacking the tarmac.

Facing backward in the cart, I could see the bog and the heather and the few bushes along the road moving past us until they came to a stop and took their place on the landscape. When the Fairy Tree sailed past, I blessed myself against evil spirits and remembered it was near here that Uncle Jack saved a woman on a dark night by filling the dry tank of her carbide lamp with his personal water.

When we arrived in Marbra, the animals jogged down the main street and the shrill whinny of the unseen stallion blanketed the town as he caught scent of the approaching mare. The mare jerked her head up, cocked her ears, and she answered the stallion with a lip-flapping love call of her own.

By the time Dad wheeled in under the arch leading to Ramsbottom's yard, the entire town knew from the urgent whinnying that the equine couple would soon behave like animals.

To save the stable door from destruction by furious hooves, the stallion's handler had already brought him out into the yard. When the stallion saw the mare, he shot up onto the rims of his hooves and danced in the gravel; his tail lashed his body, the air swishing through the coarse hairs sounding like the swish of my teacher's punishing cane. Through his nostrils his breath came out in loud, wet snorts; he trembled violently; he whinnied shrilly; he shot out a handful of steaming dung; he frothed at the mouth; his ears were erect; his eyes bulged and flamed; and his black pizzle telescoped and threatened to touch the ground two feet beneath his belly.

Quickly, Dad and I exchanged animals. I leaped out of the cart and led the pony over behind a high wooden fence. Then to keep the stallion from galloping through and mounting the wrong animal, I hasped the heavy gate.

Dad unknotted the reins and held the mare by the winkers. The mare drooled, trembled all over, danced her rear end at the stallion, and lashed herself with her tail like a Spanish penitent in a Lenten procession. With almost inaudible sighs, so high was the register, she answered her lover's whinnies and dangled her rear end toward his face. Still separated by about thirty feet the two animals drove each other to the edge of solitary release.

"Now, JohnJoe!" the handler called.

Each man freed his animal and fled to safety. The stallion was a runaway train. Shrieking and head tossing, eye-bulging and frothing, spittling and bare-toothed, with mane and tail flouncing, he galloped to the mare and bit her in the right flank with his long grassy teeth and sped on his way, his huge scrotum swinging.

His bite was rewarded with a two-hoofed kick that would have permanently maimed him if it hadn't missed. Both animals screamed. The stallion made a short turn, came back with a nip to the mare's left flank. This time the mare made only a halfhearted buck while keeping her rear hooves on the ground. By the time the galloping stallion had made a quick turnaround, the mare had spread her legs. With his tail stiff behind him, the stallion charged back to his prize.

The instant the stallion's front hooves landed on the mare's back, the handler ran across the yard and pulled the mare's tail aside. Then the stallion pushed, and the tips of his rear hooves dug into the yard's graveled surface. When every shred of his body came together to blast forth his essence, the mare anchored herself against the ferocious, primal lunging that was about to assail her.

Lunge, lunge, lunge, lunge. And then the stallion fell asleep. His head dropped down onto the mare's neck; his tail collapsed. Eventually the mare moved forward and the stallion's front hooves hit the ground. He jerked awake, looked around as if he'd just been whacked between the eyes with a sledgehammer.

Dad paid the handler half a crown, but we had to wait for an hour before setting off for home. Before her six-mile trot back to Laragh, the mare's body would have to absorb her sire's love offering. So Dad and I walked into the town, where he bought a half pound of sugar-coated cashews the size of crows' eggs, but colored like small birds' eggs—speckled blues, browns, and brown-speckled whites. He gave me four.

"Don't gobble them, Tom. That's all you're getting."

But on the way home, before we came to the Fairy Tree near Whelans of the Bog Road, Dad nudged me in the back. He handed me two more sweets.

By the time Whiteface's foal was born I was a year older and had put two and two together. But I couldn't imagine how a man and woman managed to mate, especially if the man kept biting the woman and the woman kept trying to kick the man.

❧ 30 ❧

THE BULL ON THE FARM

Dad always kept a bull on the farm. Long before the bull became too infirm to mount a cow, Dad chose a likely replacement from among his calves. For a couple of years, in preparation for licensing by the Department of Agriculture, he took special care of the lucky animal, feeding him a concoction of bone meal, milk, eggs, and oats, and taming him with regular handling and currycombing.

The language surrounding the love lives of cattle was colloquial. A cow in heat was "bulling" and she was brought to the bull to be "bulled." Neighbors drove their bulling cows to our bull, and Dad charged them half a crown for the service. If a cow would not "stand"—if she had not fully reached the state of estrus—she was left in one of our sheds overnight in the hope that by morning she would be ready for romance.

When I was eleven, Dad told me to drive one of these lodgers across the pasture to the Bog Field, where our bull was kept. "Keep a close eye on them, Tom," he said, "and be sure the bull does the job."

I trapped the cow in a corner of the field and soon the bull came trotting and lowing in anticipation. Dad said a bull could smell a bulling cow from three miles away.

When he reached the cow, the bull sniffed and snorted and poked. He raised his nose and twitched it until his nose ring was standing above his nostrils; he was like a circus seal balancing a ball. The cow played her game by lashing her tail, by shooting estrogenic perfume in his face, and by shuffling her pelvis.

Bored with watching the same old dance, I picked up three stones, and by the time the bull had done his duty I had taught myself how to juggle.

When I brought the cow home to the farmyard Dad said, "Did the bull lunge and grunt and moan when he was up on her?" This was Dad's way of asking if the bull had done his duty.

The Department of Agriculture had to examine and approve any new bull before he could be assigned to insemination duty. If the bull passed the test, Dad was instructed to put a ring in its nose before letting it loose in the fields. He was then given a license for which he paid fifteen shillings. But if the bull failed, he could not be let loose among other cattle until he'd been castrated.

There was always tension in our house on the day the inspector was to come to the farmyard. Dad knew that the careful feeding and special care he had bestowed upon the candidate could be negated with the stroke of a pen.

When the Department man arrived in his spotless overalls he poked the young bull in the ribs, looked at its eyes and teeth and ears, felt the testicles, and slapped the animal on the back several times. During the inspection Dad had his forefinger and thumb in the snorting nostrils, squeezing the nasal cartilage. Uncle Jack kept the bull's tail twisted with sufficient torque to keep its owner aware that if he moved at all, real pain was just a fraction of an inch away.

Only once did our bull fail the test. When the inspector had departed, Dad said, "Bastard! Ribs too close, and he measuring with a bloody ruler. Feckin' college man! What does he know about bulls?"

The bull had to be castrated. Fresh straw was spread on the middle house floor and the unfortunate animal was driven in. It was here he would lose his brief and never-used manhood.

With the official naysayer's rejection flaming in his brain, Dad fiercely sharpened a cut-throat razor on a piece of oiled roofing slate in the boiler house. Meanwhile Uncle Jack made a clamp by splitting a short piece of ash stick and notching the pieces to keep the tying string from falling off. Eddie was sent to the car shed for the Jeyes Fluid. I was sent to the stable to unknot the reins from the rings of a horse's winkers.

When all the tools were assembled for the removal of the testicles, Uncle Jack, like a hero of old, went into the middle house by himself. The door was hasped on the outside. Scuffling and grunting were heard until Uncle Jack finally called, "All right, JohnJoe." When Dad and Eddie and I cautiously entered, the patient was on the floor on its side, Uncle Jack was lying across its neck, his fingers in its nose. The bull's snorts were threatening, and its eyes were popping. Dad tied the rope around the front and rear legs, then pulled both sets together and secured them on the animal's belly.

"All right, Tom . . . when Jack twists him onto his back, lie across his neck. Eddie, you hold the rope between the feet and don't let him turn onto his side."

I carefully changed places with Uncle Jack, and he stepped to the rear of the bull to assist Dad.

"Get ready now, lads," Dad said. "I'm going to cut the bag."

The bull didn't react much nor did it respond to Dad's tying on the clamps that would stop the bleeding after the next wield of the razor. But when he severed the testicles from their anchors, the bull groaned like a footballer kicked between the legs. As he lifted his head off the floor, he made a sound like "Ooof!"

"Careful now, lads! When I splash on the Jeyes Fluid he's going to plunge."

The bull roared a bawl of anguish. As the stinging and burning disinfectant assailed his raw wounds, he violently strained against the ropes. But Eddie and I held our positions until the animal gave a full-bodied shudder and relaxed.

Later, as we drove the new bullock out of the middle house to the pasture, its lowing had a different timbre than before.

When I returned to the farmyard, Dad called me to the middle house. He pointed to the bovine jewels lying in the straw. Then he said, "Bury them yokes deep in the dunghill so the sows don't root them up and eat them."

ONE SPRING WHEN our bull qualified for insemination duty, the inspector reminded Dad that a nose ring had to be inserted before the bull would be allowed in the fields. The ring is a safety device. Once the nose ring is grabbed, even the most antisocial bull can be led by the nose, even by a child.

Dad considered the nose piercing a do-it-yourself job; a visit from the vet was costly. So the animal was driven into the middle house where a small window in the back wall would play a role in the insertion. The window was normally used for flinging used straw bedding out onto the dunghill in the haggard. At this time of year, the evenly spread-out manure was three feet deep and not far from the bottom of the middle house window.

Dad had a plan. Uncle Jack would fit a halter over the bull's head, tie a rope to the halter, and then throw it through the window, where Dad and I would be waiting outside. We would pull and Uncle Jack would shove until the bull's head was resting on the windowsill. Then Uncle Jack would come outside to help us keep the head steady. Meanwhile, Eddie would be in the kitchen reddening the lone tine of a broken pitchfork. He would come running out to the haggard with the tine and jump up on the dunghill when Uncle Jack gave his fierce whistle through his teeth.

So with the bull positioned for the surgeon, Eddie came galloping. He handed the fork to Dad. While directing the tine toward the cartilage in the bull's nose, Dad accidentally touched the edge of the nostril. The bull snorted and snotted, his eyes bulged, and he jerked on the rope. We pulled back. I wasn't afraid though, because Dad and Uncle Jack were there. Again, Dad tried to pierce the cartilage, but this time the bull plunged foward.

"Let go of the rope!" Dad yelled. The bull reared up and put his front hooves on the windowsill. Then he launched himself off the middle house floor. The four of us stumbled backward and into each other and we all fell.

"Run! Run away," Dad shouted and we took off in four different directions.

From my hiding place at the corner of the hayrick, I saw the bull lunging forward until he could grab onto the dunghill with his front hooves. Then he dragged his body through the window, fell on his face, jumped up, curled his tail over his back, swung his scrotum, and gave several murderous snorts.

Dad was now standing beside the Lady's Finger apple tree, waving and shouting to distract the bull and give us time to escape into the farmyard. There Uncle Jack, Eddie, and I began to laugh, and Dad smiled the smile of the naked man impaled on a cactus who said, "I thought it was a good idea at the time."

Dad sent me on my bike to get the vet. After two failed attempts to put in the nose ring, the vet had to tranquilize the bull.

✂ 31 ⚮

ACCIDENT NEAR TULLAMORE

When I was twelve, Eddie and I went with Dad to Tullamore in the pony's cart, the three of us sitting on the cross-board that acted as the seat. I sat in the middle. Red, the pony, was between the shafts. Even though Tullamore, in County Offaly, was only twelve miles from Laragh, I had never been there, and I was looking forward to seeing its canal with streets and houses on each side; the canal in Mountmellick ended just outside the town and was surrounded by fields. There was even a lock in the Tullamore waterway and I hoped we would see a barge going through it. But I don't remember if we ever got there.

Somewhere during the journey we felt a tiny hesitation in Red's onward charge, and the pony's ears swiveled forward like weathercocks sensing a new and startling breeze. I had been around horses and ponies long enough to know that when the ears went on alert, it was a signal to the driver to tighten his grip on the reins.

"There's something . . . ," Dad said, and then we heard the faraway hum of a sawmill's blade. Every time a new piece of timber passed through the mill, the unburdened blade sped up and whined to a pitch beyond the range of the human ear. By the time Dad brought

Red down to a trot, the pony was trembling. We drove around a corner on the deserted, high-hedged road, and about half a mile away we could see men working around a mobile mill, the smoke from the tractor's engine chugging into the air. Red came to a halt and began a nervous dance on the tarmac.

"Hold that tight," Dad said, passing the reins to Eddie. Then he jumped out of the cart and strode to the pony's head. He stood in front of Red, stroking his neck and muttering sounds of assurance.

"They see us, Dad," Eddie said. "They're waving." As he spoke the sound of the spinning blade sank into the countryside and became silent. The tractor's engine had been turned off.

"Wave to them, Tom. Take off your cap and wave it to make sure they see you."

Dad stayed with Red. With the ring at one end of the bit in his firm grasp he had more control over the pony.

In the distance, we could see the cigarette smoke rising from the workers at the mill. As we passed them, Dad called out, "Thanks for stopping the machine, men. The pony's a bit flighty."

"No bother, mister," one of them said. "You gave us an excuse to have a smoke. We'll wait till you're out of sight."

With Red finally calmed down, Dad climbed back into the cart and sent him into a fast trot. Then, without warning, Red took off as if he'd heard a squadron of botflies coming in for an attack; the saw had started up again.

Dad tried to bring Red under control. But the pony swerved to the right, the wheel went up onto the foot-high bank, the cart turned over, and the three of us went flying out onto the tarmac, Dad still holding the reins.

I was lying on my back on a grassy bank beside the road when I woke up. I don't remember anything else about that day except Dad was so upset at having lost control of the pony that he gave Eddie and me a half-crown each not to tell anyone about the mishap.

Long after Dad died, I asked Eddie what he remembered about the accident. He said, "That never happened. You must have dreamed it."

Dad has now been dead for forty years. I don't believe he would mind me writing about our Tullamore trip. He might just say, "That Red! He was a great pony, but it's a wonder he didn't kill us all that day."

32

ISAAC'S TREE

Dad often referred to Isaac Thompson's farm as Brodie's because Isaac's aunt, an elderly spinster named Belle Brodie, had lived there all her life. She bequeathed the farm to her nephew on condition that he come and live with her until she died. But shortly after he took up domesticity, Isaac indicated sourness had entered the relationship between himself and his aunt. One day he and Dad were chatting over a hedge when Isaac said, "I was my own man before I came here; now I'm as independent as a pig on ice." When Isaac came home late on Saturday nights with a bellyful of beer, he slept in the hay shed to avoid Belle's scolding. "There's nothing as bad as having the face et off ya when you're happy on a few pints," he said.

Old Belle eventually died and when Isaac got married, Mam became friendly with his new wife. Farm machinery was loaned between the two farms, and at harvest time Dad, Eddie, and I worked in Isaac's hayfields. He always gave us boys ten shillings each, and we were brought into his house at the end of the day for a feed of ham, mustard, brown bread, and tea. Dad did not stay for the meal. "I've the cows to milk," he'd say.

Whenever Eddie and I sat at Missus Thompson's table, a fat grey cat roamed the tabletop, its tail pointing at the ceiling and its anus on full display. In Dad's world, cats lived outside and kept the mouse population down. Besides giving our three farmyard felines a bowl of milk in the cow house each morning and evening, Dad had no love for cats. When I got older, I realized it was the shameless cat on the Thompsons' table that had sent Dad home to the cows.

Eddie and I also helped Isaac with cutting his turf. Turf was also called peat, but none of us used that word lest we be accused of being posh and "having notions."

On the bog, Isaac cut the sods of turf and slung them to me. I clamped my hands on each end of the sod to keep it from breaking in the middle and I built a twenty-five-sod pyramid on one of the side-less wheelbarrows. Meanwhile, Eddie wheeled the other full barrow out onto the bottom.

When Isaac was aboveground and needed to do his water, he went to the end of the bank and relieved himself over the side. When he was six feet belowground and had to do his water, he turned his back and peed in the corner of the bog hole he was creating. When he cut the turf in that urine-soaked area, he didn't hesitate to sling the drenched sods up to me.

When Isaac worked in our haggard at harvest time, it was he who engineered the molding of the thirty-by-fifteen-by-seventy-foot pile of hay into a rounded, waterproof shape that would withstand the water-laden wintry blasts bellowing down from Slieve Bloom. When the Angelus rang out at noon and six o'clock, Isaac leaned on the handle of his pitchfork and looked at his feet while the Catholic men took off their caps and prayed.

Five of Dad's fields abutted a twenty-acre field of Isaac's, where a small grove of trees had long ago established itself. One Sunday morning when he knew Isaac was in church, Dad went hunting rabbits in the grove and discovered a young misshapen ash tree. It had grown out of the ground shaped like the letter J. This bend indicated that the grain of the wood was curved perfectly for the making of hurleys. The bole was sufficiently thick to produce several of the sticks used in the Irish sport of hurling.

Perhaps from the age-old practice of evading the British excise man, the Irish are secretive about their wealth or the lack of it. No one would ever ask a farmer how many acres he owned. No farmer like Dad would ever admit to his neighbor that he had trespassed on his land, because the intrusion might be interpreted as snooping around.

Dad wanted the lower four feet of that ash tree, but if he asked Isaac for it then Isaac would know Dad had been walking his land. As well as that, if Isaac refused, the refusal would place intolerable strain on the relationship between the two men.

The only neighborly way to get the tree was to steal it.

One night when the moon was full, Dad interrupted our homework. To Eddie and me, he said, "I have a job for you. Put on your overcoats and your wellingtons and come out to the yard." When we joined Dad, he whispered, "We're going to cut down that ash tree of Isaac Thompson's and bring home the bottom part." My impatience at having been taken out of the warm kitchen and away from my studies suddenly disappeared; under Dad's protection we were going on an adventure in the moonlit world.

"Won't Isaac catch us?" I asked.

"We'll be quiet."

"But won't he hear the saw?"

"The wood is so fresh there will hardly be any sound."

Dad handed Eddie a rope with a horseshoe attached to one end and gave me a stout eight-foot pole of seasoned beech. In a low voice Dad said, "Voices travel farther at night. If we have to talk at all we must whisper."

Then, carrying the crosscut saw in the middle, the two ends swinging up and down like the tired wings of a crow in the evening, he led us across the Limekiln Field on the animal path until we reached the hedge separating us from Isaac's twenty acres. When Dad turned left and headed for the gate, Eddie whispered, "Why don't we take a shortcut and get over the hedge here?"

"Isaac might see our tracks in the grass and know it was us."

In single file we walked along the cart track beside the hedges at the end of the Hollow Field, the Sandpit Field, and the Rushes, Isaac's big field on our right the whole time. When we sneaked onto the Canal Line, Dad untied the piece of old baler twine holding Isaac's gate shut, and we followed him in a line through the dewy and moon-blanched grass.

I was brimming with anxiety and excitement. What could Dad possibly say if Isaac suddenly appeared? That thought made me quake, but then I realized Dad would handle any crisis like a commando in the pictures, talking himself out of a sticky situation. As our boots swished through the ankle-high grass I wished we had daubed our faces and hands with soot from the kitchen chimney.

Dad took the horseshoed rope from Eddie and threw it over a high branch of Isaac's young ash tree. When he was sure the shoe was secure he handed me the other end and said, "Stand over here, Tom, and when we start sawing keep tension on it. Once the tree begins to fall, drop the rope and run."

Dad was right about the sound of the saw in the fresh wood. I could barely hear the sharp teeth gnawing away at the damp, white meat of the tree. Back and forth the saw went from Dad to Eddie until Dad whispered loudly, "Get ready to run, Tom."

The ash tree seemed to stand tall for one last second; then the leaves and branches quivered, and unable to maintain its balance, it sighed and fell into ruins. For a moment, we stood looking down on the tree as if gazing at the still heaving body of an animal we had just killed. Then Dad organized the salvaging of the lower four feet. He pushed the beech pole under the tree and pointed to the place where Eddie and I were to saw. We knelt in the damp grass and sawed and when the blade was halfway through the trunk Dad put his feet together and lifted the long end of the pole.

We resumed sawing and Dad, by gentle increments of lifting, kept the cut from closing and locking the saw. And then we were done.

Dad tied the purloined prize to the beech pole. "Eddie, keep your feet together and you won't get a hernia," he said, and then he and my brother lifted the prize onto their shoulders. The piece of tree was a dead pig being carried home by half-dressed natives in the jungle in the cinema. I handed the crosscut to Dad and took my place at the end of the procession.

Dad gave a covetous look at the remainder of the tree. "It's a pity we can't take it all; there's great firing in dry ash," he said.

In the moonlight we trudged toward home in the same round-about way we had come. When we arrived in the farmyard, we hid the stolen wood behind a pile of stakes in the turf shed.

"If anyone ever asks where that ash came from, just say it came out of one of the fields and you won't be telling a lie."

A year later, when the ash had seasoned, Dad asked Paud Fitz to saw four hurling sticks out of the wood. But Paud cut the hurling sticks so thick that only three were produced, and the business end of each hurley—the turn of the bottom of the J—was too heavy.

"That Paud is a lazy slob," Dad said angrily. "After all our work getting the tree, he made a hames of the whole thing."

Despite Dad's bad opinion of the hurleys, my brothers and I used them to play "three goals in" in the farmyard. When we grew out of boyhood sports, our abandoned hurling sticks could be found in the corners and niches of the yard. Once I saw Mam throw one at a gourmand cat that was stalking her chickens, and Dad sometimes grabbed one in an emergency to direct an errant animal into its house.

33

BURNING BUSHES

Sixty yards down the lane from our house the Nolans lived in a three-roomed, thatched cottage. From the time I was small I toddled between the two houses. Missus Nolan was called Missus and her husband Podge.

Missus Nolan was a short, pudgy woman with bad feet. Like Granny and Missus Fitz, she dressed in black, a grey bun nestled on top of her head, not a loose hair showing. Every Sunday morning Mam drove her to mass in the small trap pulled by the black pony.

Podge Nolan, a tall man with a bushy moustache on his thin face, smoked a shiny wooden pipe that had a metal lid with holes. When the pipe went out he darted his hand into the edge of the turf fire, grabbed a small piece of live ember in his fingers, and dropped it into the bowl.

Many times when I shyly slipped into the Nolans' house, Podge entertained me with one of his tricks or inventions. He once made a twelve-inch wooden man whose limbs were attached to the body with interlocked staples. It even had elbows and knees and ankles. A dowel, about two feet long, was stuck into the little man's back.

On a kitchen chair, Podge sat on the end of a strip of pliable wood with the other end sticking out beyond his knees. When the little man stood up near the end of the strip, Podge asked, "Are you ready, Mister Dancer?" Mister Dancer answered by tapping his feet. Then Podge whistled "The Rakes of Mallow" and not only did the little man dance, he jumped up, did a somersault, and landed on his feet; he did a split, then hopped up and ran from one end of the board to the other; he stood on his head while his arms and legs flopped around; he flew into the air and spun around like the pinwheel I saw in Woolworth's in Dublin. When Podge stopped whistling, Mister Dancer began to sing, "My poor old cow all red and white I love with all my heart, she gives me milk with all her paps to pour on my rhubarb tart."

Then the little man jumped into my face and shouted, "Moo!" I fell back and Missus Nolan clapped her hands and laughed.

Whenever Podge wanted to get rid of me, he caught the cat by the tail, lifted its hind legs off the floor, looked at its arse, and said, "It's half past, Tom; time to go home."

One of the winter jobs on our farm was hedge cutting, and Dad always hired Podge to help him. Whenever he arrived in the farmyard, Podge opened the kitchen door a few inches and called, "Good morning, Missus." Without waiting for a reply, he went to the boiler house to sharpen the briar hook and billhook and the hatchet. While Dad was still milking and feeding the wintered cattle, Podge strode out to the fields with the cutting tools over his shoulder, the red-handled sharpening stone sticking up out of a pocket. By the time Dad was ready to follow, Mam had a sandwich of butter and jam ready for Podge, as well as a mug and a bottle of tea corked with a twist of newspaper.

After school, wearing damp and torn overcoats, old caps, and wellingtons, Eddie and I joined Dad and Podge. They had already thrown the heavier bushes into piles and it was our job to rake up the smaller pieces with four-grained forks. We knew that before we went home Dad would cast his hawkish eyes on the area to make sure the job had been done properly.

By the following springtime, the piles had sunk down on themselves, and the bushes had lost some of their sap. After a week of rainless days we all set out with Dad and Podge to burn them. Looking forward to burning the bushes created an adrenaline flow comparable to that of going to the circus or the pictures. Dad brought the matches, and he and Podge carried the four-grained forks. We boys argued over who would shoulder the sacks of straw; they were large and light and we pretended we were Samson before Delilah snipped off his curls.

Dad and Podge stuffed straw into several places in two piles. Then we followed Podge to watch the striking of the match and spreading of the flame in the straw. Matches were a luxury and only used on rare occasions; in our kitchen Mam used a piece of rolled-up newspaper to take a flame from the fireplace to the wicks of lamps and candles.

The men lit thin sticks off the first clump of flaming straw and carried them around to the other clumps of kindling. While we waited for the fire to get going, Podge and Dad, using their penknives, equipped each child with a wooden poker. Then Dad spent the next hour shouting, "Keep back a bit or your wellingtons will melt!"

Even though the bushes had had a week of sunny spring weather to dry out, they still contained moisture. As the hesitant flames licked their way up through the piles, they created dense dark smoke that trundled along the ground like a huge boa constrictor. We held our breath and chased each other through the wide cloud, our eyes red and burning when we emerged.

Finally, the smoke grew sufficiently hot to lift itself off the ground. In slow motion, rolling bundles rose up and up and made a giant's stairway climbing into the sky until it reached the land where Jack had stepped off his beanstalk.

As it got dark, we walked around the two circles of red-white cinders and pushed the glowing remnants toward the middle. We reddened the tips of our pokers and made heavenly halos around our heads while Dad warned, "Don't stand too close to the fire! The cold wind rushing in will give you cricks in your necks."

There were usually seven or eight piles of bushes, and the burning was stretched out over several weeks. Ashes from wood contain potash; potash is a potent fertilizer but too much of it is harmful to vegetation.

Days later, when the fires were cold, Eddie and I, each with a shovel, went to scatter the ashes. We made a game of throwing shovelfuls up in the air to watch the wind catch them and carry them off, ever thinning, like disappearing ghosts. No matter how clean we scraped the surface where the fires had been, the crops growing in the circle that year were greener and stronger than the surrounding ones. In a field of wheat or barley, the sites of the fires were islands of lushness.

One year while cutting the hedges with Dad, Podge saved a stripling of what he called the fairy bush. "The fairies make their fiddles out of it," he said. Several days later Podge presented each of us with a whistle he had whittled out of the piece of wood. "If you play the magic notes on the whistle, the fairies will leave a tiny fiddle on the windowsill," he said.

We never discovered the magic notes, but all these years later I still glance at the four windowsills whenever I visit the farmyard.

34

WE WERE RICH AND
WE DIDN'T KNOW IT

The Second World War was over and the rampant lion of the British Empire was prostrate, licking its mortal wounds. Ireland was an economic corpse.

But a silver lining lit up the jagged edges of the Irish despair: the postwar cities of England had to be rebuilt. Suddenly, jobs were to be had, and the flow of Irish emigrants across the Irish Sea became a river in full spate. Able-bodied men and women flocked to the mail boat and the ferries, while priests in the pulpit worried aloud that these innocents, facing the temptations offered by the heretical Protestant nation, would soon lose their faith. Prayers for their eternal souls floated across the water, and money for the temporal life flowed back to the emigrants' families.

The working men who stuck it out at home lived hand to mouth, mostly as farm laborers. Their bones and muscles were their tools. Many small farmers had little cash to spare, and wages were minimal, sometimes nominal, and often paid partly with a bucket of potatoes, a few heads of cabbage, and maybe a slab of bacon. There was no pay on rainy days when field work was impossible.

During this time, my farming family, living on fifty-two acres, managed to earn sufficient funds at harvest time and from the sale of livestock to pay the rates and the bills accumulated during the year for groceries, animal feed, and clothes. Given a run of two or three years of fairly good weather and good fortune, my parents were able to put some money aside for the bad times. They could afford luxuries beyond the grasp of many people, like a pulper for cutting turnips into more manageable pieces for small calves; a separator that used centrifugal force to take the cream out of milk; a pony's trap large enough for the growing family; a chemical toilet; an Aladdin lamp for the kitchen; a wind-up gramophone; and a Brownie box camera. We even had a wet/dry batteried radio whose aerial stretched high across the farmyard from the kitchen chimney to the corner of the loft.

For me the words "And now for the shipping forecast" on the BBC segued into a song about faraway places. I imagined sailors hearing the storm warnings in Utsire and Fisher, where "gale eight to gale nine winds and poor visibility" were expected. The names of places where ships sailed on the distant seas sang out amid the forecasts: Humber, Thames, Tyne, Faeroes, Viking, Finisterre, Ross, German Bight, Sheerness, Shetland, Jersey, Biscay, Shannon, the Lizard, Trafalgar, Anglesey, Dogger, Malin, Hebrides, Lundy, Fastnet, the Irish Sea.

But the radio caused as much stress as joy. The wet battery, the size of a five-pound bag of sugar, was made of heavy glass. No one in our house knew anything about the science of plates of lead and water and sulfuric acid. We just knew that the electrical charge in the battery did not last long, and therefore any listening to children's programs had to be done surreptitiously. For Dad, the radio was only for the daily news, the weather forecast at six o'clock, and GAA games on Sundays. Once when he caught me with the radio on, Dad strode across the kitchen, turned it off, and crossly said, "The next time the battery dies you'll be the one to bring it the two miles up to Padraig Scully's."

Only through distance and age have I realized how poor some of my schoolmates were, and why they believed my father was a rich oul farmer. My sandwich of buttered bread was sometimes grabbed by a townie who ran away, glancing behind like a dog making off with a bone, as he stuffed my lunch into his mouth. For years I thought those boys were bullies, but as an adult I came to understand it was hunger that drove them to their desperate acts. They weren't bullies and I wasn't their target; I was simply holding the sandwich.

As a child I believed my family was poor. After all, some of the children in the town went to the pictures far more often than we did; they had pennies to buy Peggy's Leg and Black Jack and other sweets; and they did not have to go home immediately after school to do farmwork.

We seldom went to the cinema or bought sweets because Mam and Dad said there was no money. What they probably meant was, "After such hard work to get it, you're not going to waste it." Or perhaps this was their way of keeping us from running with children they considered undisciplined. After all, we did have an aunt who was a nun, and no nun would want her nieces and nephews loose on the town.

Dad believed attending the pictures was a waste of time because it meant several hours of sitting and doing nothing. But occasionally— likely at Mam's intervention—he let us go to a matinee on a Sunday.

For me, the pictures were more than magic, more than escapism. They were real adventures in exotic and sunny lands and I was a real person in them; I grasped my wooden chair when danger appeared; I shouted, "Quick! Look behind you!"; I trembled on the edge of incontinence when the hero was sucked into quicksand; I held my breath when he struggled underwater with a crocodile; I galloped across prairies; from behind rocks I shot black-hatted cowboys; I screamed in runaway trains; I swung on vines through the jungle and wrestled with lions. How I envied the townies talking about the latest movies manned by Randolph Scott, Roy Rogers, Audie Murphy, John Wayne, and Alan Ladd. Trying to be part of the crowd, I joined in their conversation: "That detective knew all the time who the cruke was."

"It's not cruke, ya tick oul farmer, it's crook. . . . Phelan said cruke," one of the boys said.

"I did not!"

"Feck off, Phelan, and play with the other oul farmers. Oink, oink."

The townspeople had antipathy toward farmers, believing they had money hidden in their mattresses. Their belief was probably reinforced by the sight of our pony-and-trap taking the family on a drive on Sunday, four of us facing the other three on the soft, cushioned seats, a blanket spread over our laps to keep us warm. High-spirited Red, speeding along in the shafts of the rubber-wheeled, brass-appointed trap, certainly projected an air of wealth. Those Sunday outings were happy times; they allowed Dad to escape from the farm for a few hours, peer over hedges to see what other farmers were up to, and to spend time with his family. I imagine Mam was instrumental in pushing for these trips to force Dad to relax. When we arrived home after a Sunday jaunt, Dad still had to milk five cows and we all went back to the business of operating a small farm as automatically as players on a football team taking their assigned places on the field.

Compared to many of my contemporaries, I came from a rich family. But the material things and the good times this richness allowed came at the cost of incessant work.

❧ 35 ❧

THE RAMBLER

In the dark ages of the 1940s and 1950s—rural electrification was not yet universal—many localities in Ireland had ramblers, people who visited certain houses in their neighborhood on a regular circuit. In most cases the ramblers were lonely single men in search of company, gossip, and the million-to-one chance of meeting a willing woman.

Certain ramblers were welcomed, others were tolerated, and some were actively disliked. Perhaps the unpopular ones were too free with gossip, forcing the hosts to continually edit what they said; maybe they brought in clumps of cow dung on their boots; perhaps they talked too much or said too little; perhaps they used their hand instead of a handkerchief or didn't button up their trousers; maybe they spat into the fire or farted with impunity. These ramblers had been so isolated all their lives that they failed to notice the social cues that to anyone else would have been like a thunderclap exploding in the kitchen.

By trial and error, the ramblers had determined which houses were most receptive till eventually they felt comfortable enough to knock on a particular door at half-past seven on a Sunday night. So regular were the ramblers that their hosts anticipated the visits and worried if their guests did not appear, most likely sent a child the next morning to make inquiries at the house of the missing.

Many ramblers joined in playing cards with their hosts, each winner putting a penny into the paraffin box to pay for the night's supply of lamplight. The rambler never left the house without being served tea and jammed and buttered bread, even if he had won every game of Twenty-Five and was weighed down by a pocketful of enormous copper pennies.

If any ramblers had ever tried to dip their toes into my parents' hospitality, they would have found that Dad easily tired of conversing, and in less than an hour took off his boots and filled the hot water bottle. But in the case of Delia Delaney, Mam's warm welcome outweighed Dad's aggrieved hints. Mam had known Delia as a child in Derrycloney, and she had empathy for the woman. In her ferocious, hungry, lonely, despairing nonstop chatter, Delia repelled the very people she tried to befriend.

Delia, who was always old to me, was one of the farming community's unfortunate single women, condemned by the Fates to live with her unmarried brother Seamus. Side by side they worked in the fields of their fifty-acre farm, milked their cows, forked out the dungy and watery bedding from the animal houses, castrated their calves, ate together, and shared all the details of daily living. Every morning, Delia carried her brother's commode out to the dunghill and emptied it, rinsed it under the farmyard pump, and then made his bed. Farming men did no work inside the house, yet farm women often did as much work in the fields and farmyard as their men did.

Delia was a skinny woman with the sparse brown hair of a coconut that has spent too much time in the sea. She was bent at the shoulders and there was no bulge of bust. Her lips were thin and her teeth slightly bucked; her nose was as sharply humped as the Canal Bridge; her eyes were remarkable because her fair eyebrows were invisible. Her hands, battered and torn by years of wresting a living from the soil, were mindful of a turkey's scaly claws; she'd never had an unbroken nail.

The moment Delia seated herself at the kitchen fire across from Mam, she began to talk, and unless Mam forcibly interrupted her, she did not cease until she looked at the clock at eleven and said, "Sure I'd better get going. Seamus will be asleep in front of the fire waiting for me to make his cup of tea."

No matter what she talked about there was an edge of anger, of begrudgery, on the words she was so eager to get out. There were no full stops, commas, semicolons, or paragraphs. She spoke about the weather, farming, recent deaths, people from her childhood, the local scoundrels, and the people who were too high and mighty.

"And, Nan, will there ever be an end to the church building fund? Isn't Father McCluskey a terrible cranky old man? We've heard nothing but the building fund for the last twenty years. A body would feel like never giving another penny to that man. And he with two motors, one from France, Seamus says. That man does nothing but fish, and the rest of us looking for a wisp of soft grass under a hedge to wipe ourselves."

If she ever confided in Mam about her living conditions or her disappointments in life, Mam never said. Nor did Mam say Delia was ever critical of Seamus. But one time Mam told us Delia had cried while talking about her other brother, William, a member of an order of teaching brothers who worked in India, who had been home on a six-month break.

"Nothing was good enough for him, Nan. Everything was better in India. And after whitewashing and thatching and blue-stoning the windowsills and buying a geranium. And Nan, we fattened six big bullocks last winter and bought him a Morris Minor to drive around in. And when he had the attack of appendicitis he made us bring him to the Mater Hospital in Dublin because he said the one in Marbra is dirtier than the ones in India."

She and Seamus had gone in the Morris Minor with a bag of fruit to visit William in the Mater, and when they arrived in the ward, Delia had fainted, collapsed on the floor. "Not a leg under me, Nan! And the nurse said it was because I was wearing my head scarf on a hot day that stopped the heat from getting out of my body. Did you ever hear the likes? And me wearing a cap on the hottest day of the year and I never fainted before. It was the stairs, Nan; the stairs. They wouldn't let us use the lift. I thought we'd never stop climbing."

When Delia had been revived by the nurses and all the fuss was over, William in the bed told her she smelled like the farmyard and didn't know how to dress. " 'Wearing that blessed wool coat summer and winter, and that head scarf . . . no wonder you fainted,' he said."

Then he told Delia never to visit him in hospital again.

Delia cried at our fire. I imagine Mam wept, too, when she heard of William's cruel and snobbish humiliation of his sister.

At the end of the evening visit, Mam gave Delia a mug of tea and slices of the Sunday currant cake. Then she helped her into her woolen coat and escorted her out onto the lane. Delia took hold of her bike's handlebars as if they were the horns of a bull calf she was about to wrestle to the ground. A gust of wind howled around the two women as Delia switched on her flash lamp and turned her bike in the direction of home.

"Sure, Seamus says I'm as tough as an old galvanized bucket, Nan. I'll be home in no time because once I get on the Commons Road the wind will be in my back."

And then, like a lone, lost crow blown across a stormy sky, Delia was gone.

36

LUCKLESS LAR

Lar Dixon was a lonely, shy, and quiet man in his twenties who lived fifty yards beyond our house. Orphaned as a small boy, he spent his early years being handed off to different relatives. His education had been sorely neglected, and reading and writing were beyond him. When he came of age, he took over the small farm his father had bequeathed him.

Lar seldom got up before noon unless his cow bawled to have her painful udder relieved. But it wasn't the cow's discomfort that motivated Lar; it was her broadcasting to the neighbors that he was still in bed.

Mam was fond of Lar and had a lot of maternal compassion for him. Whenever it could be done without hurting his pride, she gave him his dinner. She often sent a child out with a plate for him after Dad had gone back to the fields. If Lar had spent a day selling an animal at the Mountmellick fair, Mam saved him bacon, potatoes, and cabbage and kept an eye on the lane to intercept him on his way home.

When Dad hired Lar for a day's work on our farm, Mam sent one of us children out at half-past seven to knock on his bedroom window. She hoped to save a tardy Lar from Dad's sarcastic tongue.

Once, while helping Dad to reverse a cartful of mangels into the boiler house, Lar caught his hand between the axle and the wall. Mam took care of the wound. For several weeks, Lar's hand, along with the bandage, was soaked in warm water, and a new dressing was applied. Every time he left, Mam lamented the thinness of his body and its slowness in repairing itself. In wintertime, his triple-socked feet were always cold even though he stuffed his wellingtons with newspaper he got from Mam.

Lar sometimes worked in our tillage fields with our horses. Because of this familiarity with the animals, Dad didn't hesitate to be a good neighbor whenever Lar needed to borrow a horse. He always asked Dad a few days in advance if Lame Mare would be available.

On the morning the horse was needed, Dad went out to the Back of Fitzes rattling a handful of oats in the bottom of a bucket. Then he tackled Lame Mare and tied her to the hinge of the boiler house door. But Lar never came for the horse before one o'clock.

Dad complained loudly about Lar's behavior. "That fellow! You'd think he'd be here by now, and he knowing the mare is waiting for him since morning."

Still, every time Lar asked, Dad got the horse ready first thing, Lar never arrived until afternoon, and Dad groaned.

"The sun'll be setting soon," he would say.

Lar would only smile.

When I was about nine, Lar finally saved enough money to buy his own horse. One day Lar turned him loose to graze in a field where a plough had been carelessly left. That night, perhaps frightened by something in its own imagination, the horse galloped into one of the plough's wooden handles. It sank deep into the right side of his chest. When Lar heard the wounded animal's screams, he managed to walk him home, where he died in Lar's tiny stable, originally built to house a donkey.

When my brother Eddie and I went to see the dead animal, he had collapsed against two corner walls, his terrified eyes wide open, his long yellow teeth bared in raging pain. We watched as Dad used chains and Lame Mare to drag the corpse out to the nearest field for burial. It took a long time for the child I was then to bury the frightening image of the horse's face.

"Poor old Lar," Mam often said. "He's not had one good day in his life."

Lar died in his forties. Whenever I'm in Ireland, I stand by his grave, remembering the time he had a swollen jaw from a bad tooth as well as a pronounced limp from broken toes. I was a young teenager then. For a laugh at his expense, I quipped that Lar had hoof-and-mouth disease.

The things we regret.

THE MAN WHO
KNEW EVERYTHING

For all the years I knew him, in fair or foul weather, our distant neighbor Durt Donovan dressed in a beltless gabardine coat that had witnessed the birth of many a calf; it had been worn while he examined a variety of animal orifices; it had been present at the castration of calves and at the daily milking of cows. His paddy cap, with its peak broken in the middle, was used as a glove while he handled boiling pots and kettles, as a basket to carry eggs or transport newborn kittens, and as a rag to wipe animal dung off his face.

Only the lower part of Durt's wellington boots had ever been cleaned—accidentally, when he walked through ankle-high dewy grass. The cloth of his trousers, their legs stuffed into the top of the wellingtons, had been stiffened by years of milk spillages, splashes of bovine urine, and dirt in a thousand manifestations. In a million years, the same trousers would be a paleontologist's lode, with their compressed layers as evidentiary as the Burgess Shale.

Above Durt's lantern jaw, his forehead was furrowed, and the furrows were like miniature potato drills, with farmyard manure already teased out along them, ready for the reception of seeds. His sagging neck was mindful of the loose flesh swinging at the throat of an old plodding bull.

Looking out on the world through omniscient eyes and speaking with the assuredness of the infallible pope, Durt would address those who had the misfortune to encounter him. Whenever Dad saw him coming in the distance, he climbed through the nearest hedge and hid.

One spring, I was spike-harrowing in Conroy's Field with Lame Mare and Whiteface. My brother Eddie was cutting back the previous year's briars, which had snaked their way out of the hedges and into the clay. Durt Donovan, who had his nephew Packie and Packie's pregnant wife, Monica, living with him, suddenly appeared at the whitethorn hedge beside the lane. There was no escape for Eddie and me.

Durt summoned us over. Without preamble, he addressed us across the low hedge. "Dey took yer wan"—meaning Monica—"to the hospital last night to have her babby. Hospital, me arse! In my day a woman took a batter of flour and water when she went to bed and the next morning she put the babby from her like a snot."

Having spoken ex cathedra, he adjusted his cap, uttered not another word, and processed up the lane, picking his teeth with a thorn from a gooseberry bush.

Once, when I was fourteen, I met Durt Donovan on our lane as I was riding my bike home after serving mass. The smell off him was fierce.

"I hear yer an altar bye now, chappie."

"Yes," I said, and continued pedaling until I emerged from his cloud of stink.

"I hear you're goin' off to college in September."

"I am," I said. I braked, put my foot to the ground, then twisted on the bike seat to look back at him.

"Schooling won't change who y'are, chappie. Look at me . . . I never got beyant fourth class, and I can talk with the best of them, teachers and bank managers, and I know more than the whole lot of them together." He paused for a moment. "And what will you be doing when yer finished in college?"

"I'm going to be a priest."

"A priest! Well for you! Nothing to do all day only play golf with the big nobs; eating the best, drinking, too; warm and clean all the time with a woman to buy the food and cook for you, and you not having to marry her. Grand life. But still and all, a lot of them fellas turn into contrary old shites, all thorns and no flowers. Mark my words, chappie: if you become a priest, you'll be sorry in the long run."

He walked away.

I felt resentful toward Durt for squeezing my balloon while everyone else was keeping it inflated. But as I grew older I remembered the pebble of doubt he had placed in my boot.

38

WASTED ON THE BOG AIR

Uncle Jack eventually left our house and went to live with his sister Meg and her family. He would spend the rest of his life working a hand tool for the Laois County Council. When he died four decades later, he bequeathed thirty-seven pounds and fifty pence to me and each of my siblings; his thoughtfulness, his affection, and his love were the most precious part of the gift.

Shortly after Jack's departure, one of Mam's other brothers, Paulie, moved in with us. Perhaps his sister Peg, still living at Mam's home place with my grandfather and Paulie, was fed up with two snarling, demanding, self-absorbed alcoholics and asked Mam if she and Dad would take in Paulie for a while.

I imagine there were conditions attached to his lodging with us. Dad and Mam were Pioneers and had never tasted alcohol, and Dad especially had an unforgiving attitude toward men who squandered their income and their lives on drink, particularly married men with children.

If he'd had any educational opportunities, Paulie might have soared in academia. His extraordinary memory alone would surely have boosted his skyward climb in several fields. But the times and the circumstances were not favorable, and so his intellect, like that of so many of his contemporaries in Ireland, was wasted on the bog air. At age eighteen he had his first glass of porter, at Mam and Dad's wedding reception. It was the start of a lifelong addiction. For the rest of his days, except for a few valiant Lenten efforts to remain sober, he drank whenever he had a few shillings.

Paulie once had a relationship with a woman—chaste, I imagine, in keeping with both the mores of the time and the lack of contraceptives. But his girlfriend eventually gave him a choice: "It's me or the drink, Paulie." He could not promise he would stop drinking.

Before he came to stay with us, "drunk Paulie" stories were grist for the town's gossip mills, all of them funny except to the people directly affected by his behavior. Mam winced at every tale she heard. "What a wasted life!" she'd say.

For the first couple of months he lived with us, Paulie seemed to have his liquor intake under control. But then one night in the dense dark of the unlit countryside, he waddled along our lane on his bike after drinking himself stupid in the Hill Bar.

Half a mile from our house he rode off the lane into Rourke's Drain, fell eight feet into fourteen inches of mucky water, and landed on his hands and knees. He stumbled around for a while in the Stygian blackness, fell over his bike several times, and finally, when he failed to establish his whereabouts, sat down with his back to one side of the drain. He slept till sunrise, then dragged his lower body out of the sucking muck. It was the shape of a large and familiar whitethorn bush above him that helped him get his bearings. Recovering his bike, he pulled it along the drain until he reached a right-angle turn and saw the underside of Rourke's Bridge. He found the place where we children climbed down to make echoes on our way home from school.

Instead of entering our farmyard through the wicket door and risk waking my parents, he sloshed into the garden and went into the car shed by its back door. In the shed, he removed his shoes and socks and the rest of his clothing. Hungover, naked, and spattered with mud, he stepped into the farmyard, slipped into the kitchen, tiptoed through a room with two sleeping children, and got into his bed.

When we arrived home from school that afternoon, my sister was sent up to Doctor Cosgrove's house with a note. Paulie was sick.

Doctor Cosgrove arrived two hours later in his black Austin Minor and parked in the middle of the lane outside the wicket gate. Cosgrove, a former rugby player, was a tall and gentle redheaded man. He was also drunk on arrival. When he came to the door he swayed, banged his head on the lintel, and stumbled down the two-inch step into the kitchen. He had to ask Mam to send one of the children out to his car for his bag. Mam showed him to Paulie's room and then quick-stepped out to the farmyard to tell Dad about the doctor's condition.

Dad called for Eddie and me and led us out onto the lane. Without mentioning Cosgrove's "disability," he told us we were going to turn the car because the doctor might drive into the ditch when he was leaving. Missus Fitz had fallen into the same ditch six months earlier and broken her leg.

"But he'll know we turned it and he'll be cross," I said.

"He won't even notice," Dad replied.

Dad knew nothing about motor vehicles, would not have known if the car had been left in gear or if the handbrake was engaged. Eddie was put kneeling on the driver's seat and told to turn the wheel when instructed. Dad and I took up position at the boot and pushed. The car moved forward in short jerks as if we were crossing a corrugated surface. From the rear to front, Dad and I traveled many times, with Dad whispering steering directions to Eddie every time he passed the driver's window.

We left the Austin Minor facing the town. Eddie and I ran into the haggard and climbed a pile of chopped wood so we could peep over the wall. Eventually, Doctor Cosgrove swayed out onto the lane, opened the car door, sat inside, and drove away.

The drunken doctor had told Mam that hungover Paulie had developed pneumonia. It took Paulie a week to get back on his feet, and when he did, Dad sent him packing the next day.

He had lived with us for nine weeks.

❧ 39 ❧

JIMSER SCOTT

The local church, Saint Joseph's, was a commanding presence in my young life, and the clock with its bell was the parish timekeeper. From miles away the church tower could be seen across the flat bogland.

Into the town and surrounds, the call to pray the Angelus was sent gonging thrice daily, at 7:00 a.m., noon, and 6:00 p.m. At those hours, Millet's painting *The Angelus* could be seen in *tableau vivant* on all Catholic farms. Then, if a parishioner had died, the bell would toll again, mournfully, and across hedges and streets and from donkey carts and bicycles, people would ask, "Who's dead?"

On Sundays and holy days the morning bell reminded everyone to begin the struggle into their Sunday clothes before setting out to mass on foot, on bike, in donkey-and-cart, in pony-and-trap, and by one Model T Ford with a corncrake-sounding horn that echoed the voice of its owner. "Don't laugh at him, he has no roof in his mouth," Mam said.

On Sunday mornings the footpaths became moving streams with walkers on their way to obey the First Precept of the Church:

"to respectfully and devoutly assist at the Holy Sacrifice of the Mass on all Sundays and Holy Days of Obligation." To ignore this precept meant committing a mortal sin and roasting in hell forever unless you made it to confession before you expelled your final breath. Besides the fear of eternal punishment, there was social pressure to attend Sunday mass, so great moral courage was demanded of the stay-abed. Neighbors, fearful for the soul of a recalcitrant, whispered in priestly ears, and before long a clerical visit to the sinner's home would be observed from behind lace curtains.

Through one of our farmhouse windows Jimser Scott was seen every Sunday morning biking off to mass. Jimser, a one-horse farmer, lived with his ancient mother in a thatched, whitewashed three-roomed cottage two hundred yards beyond our house. Missus Scott regularly nagged her son, "Will you go to a dance, Jimser, and find a wife? I'll polish your boots for you."

Jimser's answer was always the same. "Ah shite, mother, I can't dance."

Neither could he read nor write. After his mother was carried toes up to Acragar cemetery, Jimser spent the long winter nights alone, sitting on a wooden, straight-backed chair, looking into the fire until it went out. He cut the beaks off his hens because they were eating their own eggs. The hens soon starved to death and unsugared tea and shop-bought bread became Jimser's daily fare, except when he helped out his neighbors on threshing days and was fed a dinner of bacon, boiled potatoes, and cabbage. Once, after eating a threshing meal his stomach was not used to, Jimser threw up. One of the more witted swains said, "Jimser strained his vomit through his teeth to save the bits of meat."

When part of the roof of Jimser's "good room" fell in after a heavy rainstorm, Durt Donovan said, "Only Jimser's roof is thatched, I would say he has a slate loose."

Like his neighbor Lar Dixon, Jimser was reluctant to leave his bed before noon. But on Sunday mornings at half-past eleven, freshly shaved and wearing his polished leather boots, his Sunday suit, and his good cap, Jimser meandered along the lane on his bike toward the town for the eleven o'clock mass. At the Convent Bridge, he stopped, leaned on the parapet, and looked down into the river. He waited until the people came out of the church at the end of mass, then turned his bike and free-wheeled down the bridge to Mansfield's Pub. There, standing alone in an unlit corner, he quickly downed a pint of porter. Except for placing his order, he only once spoke in the pub, and that was to angrily say to the inattentive barman, "I didn't ask you for froth!" as he pointed to the ill-poured contents of his glass.

Because of poor eyesight, when Jimser heard footsteps on the lane or a cart approaching he sneaked into his haggard to peep out. But everyone passing by knew Jimser was on the far side of the hedge. Whenever Eddie and I went by his spy hole on our way to one of Dad's fields, we loudly said outlandish things.

"England sank into the sea last night."

"The moon fell out of the sky on Monday and landed in Durt Donovan's River Field."

Jimser, believing in the evil influence of fairies, sowed his mangel seeds in the twilight of the day of the full moon in May, when he was sure the fairies wouldn't be around. "They always go to the far side of Slieve Bloom on that night to play games and bull each other," he said.

One day, when Jimser's mare lay down in her stable and couldn't get up he sent out an alarm to the neighbors. "Me mare's down! Me mare's down!" Unless a collapsed horse is urgently brought to its feet it will soon die. Such a loss to a small farmer was disastrous.

Dad, who had dealt with downed horses before, knew what limited resources Jimser had for hoisting the mare back onto her hooves. Dad didn't even have to make a plan. While he collected a ladder and two poles, he told me to grab two burlap sacks from the boiler house and to ask Mam for the packing needle and the roll of binder twine from the dairy cupboard. On our way down to Jimser's he told me to be ready to hand things to the men and to run home for anything they might need. "But keep out of the way, Tom. Don't do anything brave and don't talk."

When we arrived at Jimser's stable Podge Nolan and Lar Dixon were already there. Dad sent Lar to our house for the two extra poles and the pulley wheels he had left inside the wicket door.

The rafters above the fallen mare were reinforced with the poles propping them up from below; from the ladder, Podge Nolan tied the pulley wheels to the rafters. While supervising these operations, Dad slit the burlap sacks open along their seams. Then using binder twine and the curved packing needle, he sewed the two sacks together. Lar tied fist-size stones into the corners of the enlarged sacks. Slipknots at the ends of four ropes were placed over the stone-filled corners and pulled tight. Dad recruited Jimser to help Lar pull and push the mare onto her back. Podge Nolan and Dad, on their hands and knees, positioned the sling under the mare. Then Lar and Jimser rolled the animal back. Finally the two ropes on either side of the sling were made into one and passed over the wheels of the pulleys. It was time to raise the mare.

Dad and Lar would pull on one rope and Podge and Jimser on the other—one strong and one weak man on each team. "Ready, lads," Dad said. "Don't jerk on the rope. Take it easy, an inch at a time. If you hear the rafters cracking, drop the mare. I'll count to three."

The stable darkened as Durt Donovan, with watery eyes, stiff grey hair sticking out from the edges of his paddy cap, and wearing his eternal gabardine coat, appeared in the doorway.

"Hold on, lads," he said. "You're doin' this all wrong. Let me tell ye. . . ."

The four men, like runners with their feet in the blocks, their bodies and brains in a high state of tension, ignored Durt. Dad called out, "One, two, three . . . gentle, lads, very gentle."

At first nothing happened. "If yeed only listen to me," Durt said.

Dad, as if telling Durt to feck off, sternly said through his teeth, "A little more, lads. Easy now! That's it." The pulley wheels squeaked for want of oil, and the mare's belly moved. "Easy, lads!"

The rafters groaned.

"That's not goin' to work, men," Durt said.

The mare's belly moved like a sackful of guts as she was slowly lifted. Her head hung down as if her neck had no muscles. Then, her legs slowly swung into place beneath her, and the men could feel slackness in the ropes. "Keep a steady pull, lads . . . she might stumble. Keep her steady."

"You're wastin' yer time, lads. That hure'll fall the minute ye let go of the ropes."

The mare tested her legs, shook and trembled, and raised her head. "Keep the pull on, lads," Dad said.

The animal lifted her tail, and a stream of long-imprisoned, green-yellow urine poured out of her like the flow from an over-turned bucket.

"Put your lip under that vitriol, Durt," Podge Nolan said. "It's full of great stuff for the brain." Under his breath he muttered, "You oul bollicks."

"And get out of the door, Durt. You're blocking the light," Dad said.

Jimser's mare lived four more years, but the death bell tolled for Jimser a lot sooner. When Doctor McSharry said he died of mal-nutrition, Mam was horrified. Her only experience with malnutri-tion was photographs in the *Irish Independent* of children in faraway countries with swollen bellies, ribs visible, and knobby joints beneath skin with no flesh.

"Malnutrition is not starvation," Dad told her. "All Jimser ever ate was bread; not even spuds and butter. He was like a calf fed on nothing but hay."

It was only at the wake that Dad learned about Jimser's Sunday morning pint in Mansfield's Pub.

ᕦ 40 ᕤ

BILLY

Spilling rain came one autumn and the fields were sodden. All the farmers in the country were caught with their cereal crops still on the stalk ready to be harvested, but the ground was too soft to bear the weight of a McCormick reaper. So Dad had to use its more primitive precursor, which meant that each sheaf had to be tied around the middle by hand with a straw rope made on the spot in a matter of seconds.

After a few dry days, Dad harnessed our three mares to the old mower and set out with Uncle Jack and Podge Nolan for Pillsworth's Field. Eddie went along in case the men had to send him home for a forgotten tool or anything else they might need.

Dad sat on the front seat and drove; Podge, sitting right behind him, used a wooden rake to separate the falling wheaten straw into sheaves and push them off the cradle behind the blades; Uncle Jack ran from one corner to the next in the boot-sucking mud, keeping the corners of the field clear of the sheaves so the horses and machine could turn without damaging them.

"Hupp! Hupp! Pyoh! Go on!" Dad continually talked to the

animals, urging them on with flicks of the reins when they showed signs of faltering. Foamy white sweat lathered the mares' rumps and thighs. Podge was like an Indian in a canoe in the pictures, paddling nonstop with a heavy oar. Eddie sat on a folded overcoat on the bank of the hedge.

Instead of the men coming home from the field for their dinner, I was sent to Pillsworth's with the ham sandwiches and sweet tea Mam had prepared. "Make sure you don't break the mugs or the bottles," she warned as she showed me out the wicket door.

An hour later, Mam was washing the delft in the white enamel basin when the latch of the wicket door rattled.

"Who could be coming?" Mam said. She dried her hands on her apron as she sped to the little window to peek out. But before she got there a big man darkened the doorway.

"Billy!" Mam said.

"Nan!" he said, and they shook hands while Billy was still standing on the step that Mam was always warning people not to trip over.

"I didn't know you were coming home," Mam said. When she turned around there were tears on her cheeks. Billy followed her.

He was dressed in a navy blue suit and black shoes. His tie was bright blue. When he removed his paddy cap his black curls leaped around his head like springs.

Mam pulled the wooden armchair into the middle of the kitchen.

"Sit there, Billy," she said. "It's grand to see you."

When Billy settled himself in the chair, he looked around and saw four pairs of eyes staring back at him.

"Are them the childers?" he asked.

"All except Eddie." Turning to us Mam said, "This is your uncle Billy, home from England." Then she marched us one by one to say our names and shake hands with this stranger. His hands were even rougher than Uncle Jack's. "Billy is my brother and Meg's and Peg's and Kit's and Paulie's and Jack's brother, too." Mam sat on the little hob that was Missus Fitz's roosting spot.

The children retreated behind the kitchen chairs.

"How's Mudd?" Billy asked. Mudd was our granny.

Mam gave him a look not meant for us children to notice. I sensed that he and Mam were speaking secrets over our heads. "She's all right, Billy," Mam said, and she changed the subject abruptly.

"Are you home for long?" She blew her nose.

"It all depends, Nan."

Mam gave him that look again. "It's bad, Billy."

Neither of them spoke for a long time. Mam's eyes became watery, and Billy swiped at his nose with the back of his hand.

"We'll talk again," Mam said, and she stood up, took hold of the tongs and stirred the fire into life. The ever-hanging kettle broke into quiet song. Billy quickly ran a red handkerchief around his face. Until then I had thought all handkerchiefs were white.

Mam placed two turf sods on the fire and sat back on the hob. Billy looked over at the children, "I have a new song," he said. "Will I sing it for ye?"

We children stared silently. A man singing in the house was as strange as Dad laughing out loud.

Billy cleared his throat and launched into "Noreen Bawn," a dirge about the "curse of emigration" that would have any pub anywhere in the world trembling on its foundations from the sobs and cries and table-pounding loneliness for home and the sadness for the daughter who contracted TB because she went to America to make a living and came home to die. Before he reached the end of the first verse, Billy had moved himself to tears, and they ran down his face in two streams. By the time he had left Noreen's dear old mammy weeping over her grave in a glen in old Tír Chonaill, there was a shake in his voice and Mam had disappeared from the kitchen. From my place behind a chair I gaped at Billy because I thought only children who skinned their knees cried.

Billy bent forward, pulled out his hanky again, and blew loudly. Mam slipped back into the kitchen and poured a mug of tea for her brother. Turning to the children she said, "Everyone go out in the yard and play."

She was met by a chorus of "Aw, Mam!" This uncle who sang and cried and kept a red handkerchief in his pocket and dressed in a suit and tie and new shoes in the middle of the week was too exotic to be separated from so soon.

Before Mam could repeat herself, Billy asked, "Where's the men?"

"Down in Pillsworth's at the wheat. The ground's too wet for the reaper and they're killing themselves with the old mowing machine."

"Sure, why didn't you tell me, Nan?" Billy said, and he stood up so quickly that his chair scraped on the floor behind him.

Within a few minutes I was one of the children trotting to keep up with the pied piper clad in wellingtons, old trousers, a coat belonging to Dad, and his damp hanky tied around his neck. With his wild curly black hair and ragged clothes Billy looked like a well-fed tinker.

We passed Jimser Scott's house in silence because we knew he always hid behind his haggard hedge to eavesdrop. When we reached the spot where years earlier a man had fallen dead off his bike into the drain, Billy stopped, took out his penknife, and jumped across the drain. He pulled down a stout ash sapling and nicked it where it was bent. Then with one quick jerk he snapped it off and leaped back onto the lane. As he continued toward the field he nicked off the branches until he was left with a twelve-foot pole. We each picked up a leafy branch and moved it through the air like the people in holy pictures waving palm fronds as Jesus rode by on an ass with no winkers.

We stayed outside the gate when Billy went into Pillsworth's. He stood beside the abandoned McCormick reaper, the ash pole in his hand like the soldier holding the spear after sticking it in Jesus' side. We could hear Dad shouting and could see him, too, sending encouraging reins along the backs of the horses, Podge rowing, and Uncle Jack trotting to catch up. So taken up were the men with their work that they didn't see Billy until they came to the end of the swath, and even then, Billy had to yell and wave.

As if caught in a beam of sunlight, the muddy faces of the three men lit up.

"Hey, Billy!" Uncle Jack shouted.

Dad stopped the mares, and he and Podge came off their seats.

"Good man, yourself, Billy," Podge said as they shook hands.

Dad greeted his brother-in-law. "Did you come all the way from London dressed like that?" Everyone laughed.

Their chatting was short-lived. Billy persuaded Dad to use the McCormick reaper, that he himself would keep the mares moving. "Give it a go, JohnJoe."

Soon the animals were unyoked from the mower and yoked to the long shaft of the reaper. With Dad at the reins in its high seat and with Podge and Uncle Jack walking behind, Billy talked to the mares. "Up girls! Keep her going! Come on, girls!" he chanted, and they moved forward without much effort.

When the machine was lined up for the next swath, Dad called, "Now, Billy!" He slammed the machine into gear, and the horses slowed against the sudden weight.

"Hupp hupp hupp!" Billy threatened, and he slapped each equine rear end with the thin end of the pole. The horses charged out of their hesitation, and for the next two hours he did not let them falter, his urgent *hupps* and unrelenting ash pole urging them on.

I climbed over the gate and sat beside Eddie in the hedge.

"Isn't Billy terrible big?"

"He's a giant."

When the final strip of wheat had fallen to the blunted cutting blades, Dad pulled back the main lever and all the working parts of the binder shuddered to a stop. There was silence except for the swish of the big wheel in the stubbles as Dad kept the mares moving until they reached the gate. The three horses suddenly became as limp as the stallion in Ramsbottom's yard after he had horsed our mare. Dad, Podge, Billy, and Uncle Jack gathered around the binder, and I could see the strength that each had maintained for hours leaving their bodies. Without speaking, they unhitched the tacklings from the binder. Eddie opened the gate, and the men and the animals passed through and onto the lane. He and I followed, kicking at the clumps of solid clay that had been pounded into the hollow parts of the mares' hooves with every step taken in the wet field.

After the horses had drunk their fill at the tank under the loft stairs, Billy took his turn at the tank, stripped to the waist, and washed himself. We children had never seen a half-naked man before, and we pulled aside the lace curtains in the kitchen to look at Billy soaping himself under the arms and around his chest. He dipped his head in the tank and covered his hair and face with suds, then turned to the windows across the farmyard and danced a little jig to make us laugh. Eddie carried out Billy's clothes and when Billy had dried himself he unhooked the barn door and disappeared into the darkness. A few minutes later he emerged, dressed in his finery once more.

Billy was a magnificent worker to whom no task was insurmountable, a man whose motto could have been, "We'll chance it, lads." During that visit home in the 1940s, Mudd died. After the funeral Billy returned to England, where he led a peripatetic life, working on the roads and buildings for several decades before he finally went back to Ireland. He never married.

When Billy eventually entered Saint Vincent's Hospital in Mountmellick, I could not imagine this giant of my childhood laid low by debilitating old age. I was living in New York by then, and Mam asked me to write to him. I barely knew Billy, so I wrote about the day he sang "Noreen Bawn" in the farmhouse kitchen and then helped save our wheat.

When he died my letter was under his pillow.

❧ 41 ❧

FLYING THE NEST

As my days in Mountmellick Boys School were coming to an end, I gathered my scholastic records and letters of recommendation and an application form and sent them off to Knockbeg junior seminary, a boarding school in south Laois. Father Patrick Maher, Knockbeg's rector, soon invited me to come for an interview.

In late summer, brandishing a new haircut and a new navy blue suit with long trousers, I set off for Knockbeg with Mam in Padraig Scully's motorcar. For forty miles I herded a belly full of butterflies, until the sight of the downward sweep of a tree-lined avenue toward a stately, mansion-like building launched me into a state of enchantment. As the purring motorcar floated down a small hill, we passed two playing fields, the goalposts blue and white. Close by was an odd-looking structure with a verandah, which could have been in a picture set in India with mounted troops in colorful regalia trotting by.

Not one person was in sight. Padraig drove through the open gate in the silver-painted railing and around an island of grass with a circular bed of flowers in the center. He brought the motorcar to a stop at the double doors guarded by a silver cannon on each side.

Father Maher greeted us. Tall and broad, he smiled as he said, "You must be Tom . . . and this is your mother." Even before I withdrew my hand from his, I knew he was no prickly Father McCluskey.

I had expected the rector and I would head to his office for the interview, but instead, with Mam on one side and me on the other, he took us on a tour of the school, all the time chatting and asking me questions.

"Were you an altar boy, Tom?"

"Yes, Father."

"*Introibo ad altare Dei,*" he said, and I replied, "*Ad Deum qui laetificat juventutem meam.*"

"*Dominus vobiscum.*"

"*Et cum spiritu tuo.*"

We walked through the study hall with its skylights, a line of windows on one side, and eighty two-seater desks arranged in rows.

"The roof is galvanized and when there's heavy rain you can't hear your ears, but at the same time the sound makes you feel safe and dry."

"Like when you're warm in bed and there's a storm?" I said.

"Exactly. . . . Do you read books, Tom?"

"Yes, Father."

"What were the last three you read?"

"*Riders of the Purple Sage, King Solomon's Mines,* and *Dr. Jekyll and Mr. Hyde.*"

"Which was the best?"

"*Riders of the Purple Sage.* It was sunny all the time in Utah."

Father Maher showed us the boot hall with its two rows of cubicles, each big enough for a pair of shoes. "One of our rules is that all the boys change into their black shoes before they go outside; the brown ones are for inside. This helps keep the floors clean."

"Where's the fireplace?" I asked.

"We don't have one, Tom. All the buildings are heated by hot water in pipes."

I couldn't imagine living without a fireplace. What would we all sit around when the wind was howling and the rain spilling?

I kept wondering when the interview would start.

The rector led us outside and waved a hand at the unmowed playing fields. "That green and red pavilion is where the boys dress before games."

I thought of all the times I had changed into my shorts and jerseys in the bushes beside the football field in Mountmellick, hoping that when the match was over no one would have thrown my clothes high up into the hedge.

Over a rusted-brown iron fence Father Maher pointed to the weir on the Barrow River a couple of hundred yards away. "Do you know what a weir is, Tom?"

"It's for holding back the water to make the river deep for boats."

"That's right. . . . Of course the students are not allowed beyond this fence."

We passed a large tank at the back of the ball alley. "That's where the gas for the science room is made," Father Maher said.

Then he caught me by surprise. "How is Father McCluskey?" he asked.

I hesitated for a moment, then spoke. "I served mass for him this morning. He was very nice," I lied.

Soon our tour was completed, and we arrived back at the main building. Now we'll have the interview, I thought. But instead Father Maher said, "Tom, go and ask the driver of the motorcar to come in and have tea and biscuits with us."

"Look at me oul dirty boots," Padraig said to me, as he rubbed them on the legs of his trousers. "And look at me dirty hands. I'll try to keep them in my pockets."

As we approached the door he said, "The priest must be a nice man if he's inviting the driver in. Imagine Father McCluskey asking me to his house for tea!"

Father Maher extended his hand to the driver, who said, "Me name is Padraig, Father. Excuse the state of me hand."

"A bit of honest dirt never hurt a man."

During the tea Father Maher made it easy for everyone to talk.

"Padraig, if I was going to buy a motorcar, what do you think I should get?"

"Has your husband all the hay in, Missus Phelan?"

"Has your father any sugar beet, Tom?"

"He has," I said.

"And Tom is a great thinner," Mam said. I could feel my face redden.

"Do you use a hoe, Tom?"

"No, Father. We tie sacks around our knees and crawl along on them."

"How many acres?"

"Three, Father."

"That's a lot of kneeling and thinning."

"I'm glad I'm not a farmer," Padraig said. "Too much nonstop work for me."

"Me, too," Father Maher said. "I was brought up on a farm and I spent many a day in the beet field."

When the last cup of tea was finished, Padraig returned to his motorcar, and I braced myself for the interview that would determine whether I would be accepted into Knockbeg. But instead Father Maher said, "Congratulations, Tom. You will be a member of the new class beginning on the sixth of September."

My spirits soared, but I was puzzled.

When I sat into the taxi, Mam said, "Isn't Father Maher a nice man, and he interviewing you all the time and you not even knowing?"

For the next couple of weeks, from waking up to falling asleep, I thought only of Knockbeg and the football fields, the study hall, the weir, the dormitories, the ball alley. I thought of the difference between cranky Father McCluskey and Father Maher, who spoke to me as if nothing else was going on in his world.

My family began preparing me for life in boarding school. While turning the turf on the bog with me one day, one of my sisters said, "When you're in Knockbeg, you'll have to sleep in the top part of your pajamas, not your shirt."

"You better start practicing not spitting," Dad told me. "If you spit in Knockbeg, they'll say you're a tinker. And never borrow money from anyone. If you're asked for some say you don't have any."

"Don't lick your knife."

"Always have a handkerchief in your pocket," Mam said. "Don't pick your nose."

Mam bought me a new toothbrush and a tube of toothpaste and two boxes of Kiwi polish, one black and one brown. "I won't be there to shine your shoes on Saturday night," she said. "You'll have to do them yourself."

Mam also got me a small sewing case, a nail brush, and six pairs of wool socks. She did not buy me any undershirts or underpants because at that time in farming Ireland only girls wore them.

One of my sisters held up the nail brush. "Do you see this, Tom? Use it all the time. There's nothing worse than the dirty nails of someone picking a potato out of the bowl."

"And don't wear your socks in the bed or you'll have cold feet the next day."

"The lavs in Knockbeg will be like the ones in Aunt Teresa's convent. Don't forget to flush."

Mam washed and ironed two pairs of sheets, two pillowcases, two shirts, and two laundry bags.

"Now, Tom," my sister said when we were alone, "don't be surprised if Dad is not in the yard when you're leaving in Padraig's motorcar. Mam told me he's very sad that you're going away."

Time crawled until my last day on Laragh Lane arrived. Missus Fitz brought me a bag of homemade fudge. Tears flowed down her cheeks as she shook my hand goodbye. "Just in case I die before you come home again, Tom, remember you promised you'll pray for me poor oul soul in your first mass."

Dad opened the high galvanized gate an hour before the motorcar was due. "Padraig might come early," he said.

Eddie carried my black suitcase outside and left it near the pump. I didn't know what to do with myself. In my suit and shiny shoes, I was too dressed up to do any jobs. I was too excited to sit down and read. Eventually, I went out to visit some of the farmyard houses—the car shed, turkey house, pig house, new stable, barn middle house, stable, cow house, boiler house. I pushed in the doors and just stood there, looking in. It was hard to accept that I would not be doing my jobs there in the coming winter; I'd not have to put on my old clothes until I came home at Christmas, and I was sad and happy at the same time. I couldn't imagine Dad and Mam and my sisters and brothers going on about the daily farm work without me.

I was turning away from the boiler house when my sister ran out, shouting, "He's on the Canal Line!" and within two minutes Padraig was slowly driving into the yard.

I quick-stepped out to the haggard to find Dad. But he wasn't there. I decided to look in the turf shed, and when I'd gone through the gate at the end of the yard I saw him on the far side of the pasture walking toward the Bog Field. I cupped my hands around my mouth and shouted, "Goodbye, Dad!"

He turned around and waved.

"Goodbye, Dad," I called again, and then I cried.

EPILOGUE

On a June day in 1965, I was one of thirty-two newly ordained priests processing down the aisle of Saint Patrick's Cathedral in Carlow to the triumphal music of Palestrina's "Christus Vincit"—Christ has conquered. Mam and Dad and my siblings had made great financial sacrifices to support me through the years of preparation for this day. My family was proud of me, I was proud of me. I was twenty-four, and I thought I had the world by the tail.

Eleven years later, totally disillusioned, I left the priesthood. Durt Donovan was right.

A FEW YEARS after escaping the clerical life, I strolled around the farmyard on a summer's evening. It was dry and musty and soaked in the memories of childhood. On the barn wall still hung the two slatted sideboards of a horse's cart, blue like a blackbird's eggs. The half-doors of the middle house were still hanging crooked; the same chain hung there with the big link at the end to hook onto the same piece of bent iron set into the wall. I touched the smooth link, held it between my fingers, and saw Dad and myself pulling on a rope tied to the protruding yellow ankles of a calf still inside its mother. I heard the cow moaning and Dad saying "Now!" and I felt the calf slipping and saw the cow's end stretching into a large O. I heard my brother Eddie behind me saying, "I'm ready to go, Tom."

Dad was dying. In a midnight phone call to New York, where I'd been living for a decade, Eddie had called me home to Ireland. Now we were going to Saint Vincent's, where Dad was living his last days.

It was as if he had been waiting for me, as if he knew that I had been standing outside the door. He held his arms feebly in the air, as if reaching out to take a baby.

"Tom!" he cried.

"Dad," I sobbed as we awkwardly clutched each other, my wet bearded face next to his trembling toothless mouth, the son bending down, the father reaching up, each clutching at something that had slipped out from between them and grasping at it for a fleeting moment.

I got down on my knees beside the bed and held the backs of my father's fingers against my forehead, and my sobbing body made noises in the springs of the bed. I felt my father's free hand in my hair, touching, resting there. I heard his cries, like the creaking of an old barn in the wind.

"Tom," he said eventually. "I was hoping you'd come home to rake the stubbles. You'd better use Whiteface, even though she'll drive you mad with that tail of hers, swiping at flies even when there's none to swipe. The wheel rake's over in the Sandpit Field near the gate. Be careful coming through the Hollow Field gate! It's barely wide enough—and don't forget to put the grease on the axle."

Watching my father's face, I saw the old eyes looking at the past, watched them wander all over the farm, unable to separate the layers of time, seeing people and horses in the wrong years and seasons. The words flowed out of knots of time trapped in his memory, rising inconsequentially to the surface like random bubbles floating up from the deep bottom of a dark boghole. He spoke again.

"How much time did they give you?"

"Two weeks." I got up and pulled the straight-backed chair to the bedside.

"Two weeks! . . . I told Eddie two weeks ago to move the cattle out of Pillsworth's into Conroy's. But he wouldn't listen. They'll skin Pillsworth's, and he won't have a bit of grass in the spring."

The lostness of my father's mind added to my sadness, and I bent my head to my chest. I cried as foals were born and horses died, as the rain ruined harvests and cattle broke down fences, as hay was saved and bits of football matches were replayed, as fields were ploughed and neighbors emigrated.

I left the room, and in a dark corner in the corridor I cried in silence. I did that every day for two weeks.

On my last day home, I was sitting in the wide hedge that straddled the spine of the Sandpit and Hollow fields. In the slanting sun, rabbits nibbled their way from the safety of their burrows, their noses twitching. I was staring into the hollow below when I became aware of someone approaching. The rabbits hopped, then vanished.

It was Eddie swishing his way through the tall sour grass that grew in the shadow of the hedge. I moved my hand in greeting, and Eddie checked a sitting place with the side of his boot.

I spoke first. "The last time I was home, I sat here with Dad. He fired shots at a rabbit three times—and missed. I don't think he really wanted to hit it. It was the first time he'd looked through a telescopic sight, the first time he'd seen a rabbit grazing up close."

We gazed down into the hollow, across the sheets of golden buttercups and over the hedge that separated the Sandpit Field from the Rushes.

Eddie said, "It was hard for everybody when Dad slowed down. He'd get terribly cross at himself. Then he'd get cross at Mam and me. I couldn't talk to him at all. He wanted to go to Saint Vincent's, but Mam couldn't bear to see him leave. Then you wrote and told her to let him go. That was the best letter you ever wrote. We brought him up on a Thursday evening."

A spear of breeze startled a group of buttercups.

"The next morning I went to see him, and when I was coming home I stopped in at Ned Hyland's. Ned asked me, 'Where are you going all dressed up?' and I said I'd been up to Saint Vincent's to visit Dad, and then I burst out crying. I felt like a real eejit in front of Ned." Eddie snuffled loudly and wiped the back of his hand across his nose. A half-strangled sob escaped into the thick grass.

Eddie spoke again. "That was his favorite place over there at the Beech Trees. It's mine, too. It's the nicest place on the farm. The Sunday before we brought him to Saint Vincent's, Mam came out to me in the barn and said she couldn't find him anywhere. We looked in all the houses, and then we went across the fields. When we got to the Rushes gate, we could see him sitting on the roots of one of the trees. The cattle were all around him, sniffing. It was like he had come over to say goodbye to them. To say goodbye to the whole thing. Mam went ahead and got him, and I waited there at the gate for them. And then I walked home behind them. It was terribly sad."

I started to cry. Then with great sorrow, Eddie began to sob. Together in the hedge, we wept, letting the sadness come out loudly and unashamed. Side by side in the bushes, Eddie with his head on his arms across his up-pulled knees, me looking blindly at the Beech Trees, the tears flowing itchingly into my beard.

GLOSSARY

Angelus: prayer commemorating the conception of Jesus.

arse: ass; a person's rear end.

Artisans' Dwellings: name of a Dublin construction company; the houses were built by artisans, but not for artisans.

ashplant: ash stripling with a knob on the end where it was cut off from the main plant.

ate the face off: gave a scalding dressing-down to.

beet fork: a six-tined fork with tines about a foot long, gently curved and with small nobs on the end to avoid their sticking in the sugar beet during loading.

beet knife: short-bladed machete.

beet pulp: what was left after the sugar was extracted from the beet root.

beet tops: the leaves growing out of the beet plant at soil level.

belt of a bush, tilled with the: a throwaway phrase meaning soil was so soft it could be tilled by belting, or whacking it, with a thorny blackthron bush.

blurt: fart.

bogies: low-slung platforms on small wheels, with a winch attached for loading cocks of hay.

bollicks: curmudgeon, difficult personality, pain in the arse, contrarian.

boogie man: imaginary snatcher of children.

box of the wheel: the fortified center of a wheel where the axle is inserted.

Brian Boru: high king of Ireland who defeated Danish invaders in 1014 at the Battle of Clontarf.

britchens: part of the tacklings that went over the rump of a horse and was attached to the shafts of a cart.

bull, to bull each other: to have sex.

butter paper: paper for wrapping butter or meat; wax paper.

camogie: women's version of the Irish sport of hurling.

Canal Line: the towpath for the horse that pulled a barge.

clamp of turf: wall of sods of turf, built to keep the pile of turf tidy.

clocking turkey: a brooding turkey.

crane: iron device hanging above the fire; it could be lowered or raised from the heat; several pots could be suspended at the same time from its hooks.

creels: upward extensions added to the sides and ends of a cart to allow for a bigger load.

Croke Park: main stadium of the GAA, located in Dublin.

d'arse: the arse.

delft: tableware, usually white and blue, called after the city of Delft in Holland.

dinner: main meal of the day, eaten at 1:00 p.m.

ditch: a drain running beside a hedge, usually around the edge of a field.

draughts: traces attached to a horse's collar and a singletree.

Drogheda: town in County Louth.

Dubh Linn: Irish for Dublin; literally, black pool.

dunghill: a heap of animal bedding (i.e., straw) and animal waste.

eejit: idiot.

ex cathedra: from the seat; when the pope speaks as head of the Church on matters of faith or morals, he speaks "from the seat" of Peter. In this instance, he is said to be infallible.

Fair Day: cattle market.

Fairy Tree: tree to be avoided because it is the dwelling place of fairies.

feckin', fecking: mild forms of "fucking."

followers: game played with marbles and using rules similar to those in bocce; the bowling lawn is an unending road.

four-grained fork: four-tined dung fork.

Furry Hill: furze, furse, gorse, or whin bushes grew in the field beside this hill; furzy hill became Furry Hill.

GAA: Gaelic Athletic Association, an amateur sporting and cultural association, that promotes Irish sports including hurling, camogie, and Gaelic football.

Gaelic League: Founded in 1893 with the aim of restoring the Irish language (Gaelic), the league conducted language classes throughout the country. Its optimistic aims were not achieved.

grub, to: to use a drill grub, a farm implement with seven long iron teeth irregularly placed on an iron frame. It is sufficiently narrow to be dragged by a horse between drills of root crops to disturb weeds growing in the furrows.

haggard: enclosed open-air area for storage of animal fodder and farmyard manure.

half a crown: one-eighth of a British pound; in 1952, about forty-five cents.

hames: two curved metal bars, joined by a short chain at one end, fitting into a groove in a horse's collar. Hooks on a hame allow for the attachment of traces. Because the chain joining the two bars sometimes became twisted, the expression "to make a hames of it" means to make a mess of something.

hob: a cast-iron cabinet besides a fireplace, used for warming pans and plates. The top of the hob was the seat most fought over in wintertime because of its proximity to the fire.

hoose: bovine parasitic bronchitis causing animals to cough loudly and frequently.

hure: whore. Not necessarily a woman; often applied to a man who is a son of a bitch, a mean and nasty person, or a bollicks. When preceded by "real," the word assumes hurricane strength.

hurley: wooden stick used in the Irish sport of hurling.

hurling: fast field game in which opposing teams use hurleys and a hard leather ball to score points.

IHS: *Jesu Hominum Salvator* (Jesus, Savior of Men) is one of many interpretations of this ancient symbol.

Ireland's Own: family magazine first issued in 1902.

jow: dung.

Jubilee nurse: In 1887, when Queen Victoria celebrated the golden jubilee of her ascension to the throne, the women of England presented her with a gift of seventy thousands pounds (8.5 million today). Queen Victoria used the money to train nurses who would live and work in remote areas of the British Isles.

Laois: county in Ireland's midlands. Pronounced "leash."

level crossing: railroad crossing.

mangel: mangold; large round root vegetable grown for animal feed.

Marbra: corruption of Maryborough, former name of Portlaoise, county seat of Laois.

messages: groceries; "going for the messages" was going to the town to buy groceries.

middle house: animal house between the stable and barn.

MPSI: Member of the Pharmaceutical Society of Ireland.

nappies: diapers.

oul: old; adds emphasis to the insult of being called an "oul girl" or an "oul farmer's son."

oxter: armpit.

paddy cap: peaked cloth cap; the English call it a "flat cap."

pap: cow's teat.

parish priest: pastor.

paunched: disemboweled.

pebble dashed: a wall finished in pebble dashing, an outside finish consisting of small stones embedded in mortar.

pictures: movies.

pinfeather: developing feather that still has blood in it.

Pioneer: member of the Pioneer Total Abstinence Association, an Irish religious association for people who abstain from alcohol.

pixie: girl's knitted hat tied under the chin.

plimsolls: a light rubber-soled canvas shoe.

pony-and-trap, pony's trap: cushioned, sprung, rubber-wheeled conveyance; an upscale version of a pony's cart.

pooka: most vicious being in the pantheon of Irish fairies; sometimes took the form of a horse that buried itself in a laneway, and when the victim walked over it, the pooka jumped up and took him on a wild ride to parts unknown.

Rineanna: former name of Shannon Airport.

Sacred Heart lamp: small, red-globed lamp kept alight in front of a picture of the Sacred Heart of Jesus; found in many Irish kitchens.

scald: young bird.

scour: diarrhea in an animal.

scraping mangels: the clay adhering to this root crop is scraped off just before use because any small wound would lead to quick decay.

seed barrow: seeding machine for turnips and other root crops.

shied: description of (a sometimes violent) reaction of a horse when startled or spooked; a newspaper blowing in the wind might make a horse shy.

sleeveen: nastily sly person.

Slieve Bloom: mountain range on the border between counties Laois and Offaly.

snags: short sprouts on stored potatoes.

spring-grub: farm implement fitted with four rows of "springy" steel feet that loosen the soil after it has been ploughed.

stubbles: what's left after the passage of a harvester in a field of corn.

supper: evening meal, eaten at 6:00 p.m.

tackle (a horse): outfit a horse for field work or haulage work.

that one: disparaging reference to a woman, worse than calling her "she."

tinker: originally a person who worked with tin, making utensils or mending them. The term became associated with people of no fixed abode. Today, it is considered a pejorative, and the term "traveler" is used.

townland: a small geographic division of land in Ireland. A town is comprised of numerous townlands. For the most part, their boundaries are unmarked but are known to the local people and appear on maps. There are more than sixty thousand townlands in the country.

turf: peat cut to the size of a loaf of bread, dried by the sun and wind, and used for fuel. In the days of open fireplaces about ten thousand sods of turf would be used in a home each year.

turning barley: before drying equipment was available, barley was stored on wooden floors to a depth of two feet. To keep it from "heating up" from its own moisture, the barley had to be regularly "turned." To avoid damaging the grain, wooden shovels were used.

TVO (Tractor Vaporizing Oil): basically paraffin oil with some additives.

whipping top: child's toy using a cone-like top and a light whip.

whitethorn: large bush producing a display of white blossoms in May and perfuming the Irish countryside.

wingboard: four boards easily attached to the sides, back, and front of a cart to give it more depth and hence carrying capacity.

winkers: a horse's leather bridle with sides (blinkers) attached to restrict peripheral vision and hence keep the horse from being startled.

winter cattle: cattle housed and fed and bedded during the winter.

woodquest: a woodpigeon or ring dove; agricultural pest.

yer man, your man: used when a name cannot be remembered, or used disdainfully when the name is known. "Yer man was eatin' the altar rails again with cow dung on his boots."

yoke: word applied to anything whose name is momentarily forgotten. "Hand me that yoke."

ACKNOWLEDGMENTS

Thank you to Maura Mulligan and Kate Hourigan for Irish translations and to Seamus Deegan for checking my Latin.

My gratitude to Peter McDermott, deputy editor of the *Irish Echo*, for his longtime encouragement and for publishing some of the early JohnJoe stories.

Thank you to the staff of the Freeport Memorial Library in Freeport, New York, for their unfailing and enthusiastic assistance.

I am grateful to the Tyrone Guthrie Centre in Annaghmakerrig, County Monaghan; OBRAS Portugal in Evoramonte; and the Ireland Fund of Monaco and Princess Grace Irish Library for residencies that were helpful in the writing of *We Were Rich and We Didn't Know It*.

My appreciation to my untiring agent, Tracy Brennan of Trace Literary Agency, and to editorial director Aimèe Bell, executive editor Jeremie Ruby-Strauss, editorial assistant Brita Lundberg, copy editor Shelly Perron, and the staff at Gallery Books for their efforts on my behalf.

Thank you to my sons, Joseph and Michael, for their continual encouragement.

Finally, my gratitude to Patricia Mansfield Phelan, my wife. She has been my great encourager, she has been of wonderful and patient editorial assistance, and her suggestions, despite my occasional resistance, are always on target.

ABOUT THE AUTHOR

Tom Phelan was born and raised on a farm in County Laois, Ireland. His first novel, *In the Season of the Daisies*, was published to acclaim when he was fifty, prompting one reviewer to write, "The most obvious question posed by a novelistic debut with as much resounding vigour as this is: Where has Mr. Phelan *been*?" Since then, Phelan has written the novels *Iscariot, Derrycloney, The Canal Bridge, Nailer*, and *Lies the Mushroom Pickers Told*. He lives with his wife in New York.